RUN RACHEL RUN

THE THRILLING, TRUE STORY OF A TEEN'S DARING ESCAPE AND HEROIC SURVIVAL DURING THE HOLOCAUST

RACHEL BLUM

For more info:
www.rachelblum.org
www.runrachelrun.org

This book is dedicated to the 1.5 million children
who did not escape the Nazi Holocaust
and go on to live full lives
like Rachel.

CONTENTS

CHAPTER 1

THE MOMENT OF TRUTH

July 1944

IVAN ROLUK LOOKS BEHIND HIM. THE TWENTY TRAIN CARS FILLED WITH over one thousand wounded Nazi soldiers snakes behind the engine car like a meandering river. In the caboose at the tail of the train is his wife, Maria; his son, Stephan; and the fourteen-year-old Jewish girl, Rachel. It is time to give them the signal.

He applies the brakes, slowing down the train. Then he blows the horn...once...twice...three times.

He looks back. Have they jumped out of the caboose? Or were those shadows he saw?

He hears a door slam. What is it? It sounds like the door connecting the engine to the first car, which is occupied by high-ranking Nazi officers. Is one of them coming up front?

The moment of truth has arrived. He releases the brakes and thrusts the throttle full ahead.

Ivan would never show it, but in his heart of hearts he is terrified. He loves his wife. He loves his son. He doesn't want to die.

How did he let that little Jewish girl convince him? How did she have so much courage? Where did she get it from? Why was she so sure of herself, so sure of the plan?

There's no more time for thinking. He leans out the open side door. The wind blows in his face. The ground speeds past him. He takes a step...

As he jumps, the thought keeps circling through his head: That little Jewish girl was not afraid, that little Jewish girl was not afraid, that little Jewish girl was not afraid....

CHAPTER 2

A TERRIFYING NIGHT

June 22, 1941

RACHEL IS TERRIFIED.

She always had a hard time sleeping. It didn't have to be a nightmare. It was just terrifying to be in the dark. Even with her older sister in the next bed, her older brothers in the next room, and her father in his room.

Why am I always afraid? she thinks, her eyes still closed.

Suddenly, there is a distant boom.

Rachel opens her eyes. *What is that? A thunderbolt?*

Even though her bedroom is pitch black, her eyes are already beginning to adjust. Perhaps it's because she is so used to waking up in the middle of the night.

Maybe you're just hearing things, Rachel thinks. *You're always so afraid. Why do you have to be afraid all the time?*

She looks around the darkened room. There is Hannah, sleeping soundly under the covers in the next bed. The door to the adjacent room where her brothers sleep is slightly ajar, because Rachel always insists they keep it open.

"It's comforting," she had told them.

Although she could not see more than the ends of their beds, she could see the outline of the feet and curled-up legs of her brothers: Motl, Wolf, and Simcha.

Maybe it's Father walking around the house?

He was always up before dawn. Sometimes he puttered around the kitchen — which was also the dining room and main living area — often cleaning up the mess left over from the previous night that was still out on the table. (As a widower, he often had to be a father and mother at the same time.) Many mornings he prepared the water buckets to take to the well and fill up with water.

Maybe the noise is him knocking into something or rummaging through the tool chest or bread closet, or even knocking over a book on the overloaded bookcase? On second thought, it probably isn't Father. It's still too early.

Although the Blums' house never had a clock, Rachel developed a sense of time, even when waking up in the middle of the night. In fact, she woke up so often that she knew the pattern; there were still several hours to go until morning.

She thinks about getting up and walking around, but Father had told her specifically not to do that. It wasn't good for her and it wasn't good for the others because she might wake them up — and they needed their sleep.

Sometimes she would get up anyway when she knew for certain that Father was up. She would dress and show up in the kitchen, begging him to take her with him to the well. And often he would. Especially on Sunday mornings, when most of the Poles didn't go to the well, when there was less chance that one of them would utter a hateful remark or start an incident.

But he was clearly not up. If he were, Rachel would have heard the creaks his footsteps made even when he was trying his best to be quiet. But she didn't hear one creak. No, Father was still sleeping.

Oh, you're just a scaredy-cat. Close your eyes and try to go back to sleep.

Rachel closes her eyes.

As soon as she does, she hears the distant noise again. It is unmistakable now. Like the sound of thunder. Do the others hear it?

No, Hannah is still sleeping soundly. And the boys are not stirring.

Why are you afraid of a little thunder and lightning? Do you think it'll really hit you? You're just a fearful, scared little girl. You've always been that way. Since you can remember, you were afraid. Afraid of what? Of everything. Of nothing. There's nothing to be afraid of. Just go back to sleep.

Then she hears it again. Except this time, it is followed by two, three, and four distant rumblings in succession. They are distant, but noticeably louder. The storm is obviously moving closer.

Boom! Several more thunderclaps in a row. *Boom! Boom! Boom!* There are so many that even Hannah lifts her head.

The next crack of thunder is so loud that the boys in the other room jump out of bed.

Then a shout from outside. It sounds like a neighbor. *What's he doing outside at such an early hour?*

The thunder is rolling continually and getting louder.

Boom! Boom! Boom! Boom!

Father peeks his head into the room. "Hannah and Rachel," he says, "get dressed quickly."

Why is everyone making such a fuss about a little thunder? Are they as afraid as I am? How silly of them. Don't they know the chances of getting hit by lightning are almost impossible?

But Rachel doesn't question it. She is happy that everyone is getting up. There is comfort in numbers. Her family is her life. She loves them all dearly. Even when they fight with each other. Even when they don't include her. Family is life, and now her house is coming alive. So how bad could things be?

She puts on her dress and shoes, and follows Hannah into the kitchen. The boys are already huddled together, discussing something. What, Rachel has no idea.

The thunder continues getting louder.

Boom! Boom! Boom! Boom!

You know, Rachel realizes, *it doesn't sound exactly like thunder...*

Another loud blast — *boom!* The loudest one yet, almost as if it was right outside her front door. Motl is the first to the door and opens it.

Rachel can see a gentle reddish glow outside. The day must be dawning.

"Quick, children!" Father shouts. "Everyone back to the bedroom!"

Rachel's mind instinctively flashes an image. It is a recent conversation with her father:

"Father, last night I was playing with my doll under the table and you were sitting around the table with the boys, and I heard you say something. You said that war is coming."

"Nobody knows anything for sure, my child."

"The Germans are bad people, aren't they?"

"They're just people. Before you were born, there was a war and the Germans invaded. They came into our town, but they didn't want to fight us. They wanted to fight the Russians. They wanted to stay in our houses for a night or two and have us feed them — which we did. But then they left. They stayed for only a short while before going on and fighting the Russians. Some of them were very gentlemanly about it."

"But I heard you say these Germans aren't the same Germans from the last war."

"Your brothers and I were just talking... Sometimes we do that."

"But I want to know, Father. Please. I remember exactly what you said: 'War is coming. And these Germans are not the same Germans from the last war. Their war was against the Russians. But this war will be a war against the Jews.' What did you mean by that?"

"Your brothers and I were just talking."

"I'm not a baby anymore. I'm old enough to understand things. I heard this man Hitler is very bad."

"He is, but he has a lot of enemies — including England and France, and they have the two strongest armies in the world. They're a lot stronger than him. But even if war came, who says it would come to our little town? You don't have to worry yourself about it... Nothing bad will ever happen."

Thunderous booms reverberate everywhere. Rachel realizes for the first time that they aren't the booms of thunder, but of bombs!

Bombs are falling all over. Each shell shakes the ground worse than the previous one. Outside the Blum house, on the streets of their town, Ludmir, fires began breaking out in several houses that have taken direct hits.

"Quick, children," Father shouts again. "Everyone to the big bedroom!"

Motl slams the front door and races with the others back to the boys' room. Father says, "Push all the beds together and hide underneath."

Hannah and Rachel comply quickly, and Wolf and Simcha join them under the beds, but Motl races back to the front door.

"Motl, come back!" Father shouts. "It isn't safe!"

"I have to see," Motl replies. "How much safer is it under the bed?"

Of course it's safer under the bed, Rachel thinks. *If it isn't safe here, surrounded by family and protected inside the house, where is safe?*

"All right, Motl," Father says. "Keep watch. Let us know if the fires get too close to the house."

Thunderous booms still rattle the walls. Heavy, thick smoke envelopes the streets of Ludmir. In between the bomb bursts one can hear the shouts of terror. People screaming.

As the Blums lay huddled under the beds, the bombing seems to stop. The lull restores some color to their faces. No one says a word.

Then — a distant boom.

Then a little louder one.

And a louder one.

And the loudest one yet, as if it had landed just outside the door! *Boooooooooooooom!!*

"Quick, children, pray!" Father shouts.

Rachel whimpers. There, next to her terrified siblings, she closes her eyes and prays like never before. Uttering each word of the *Shema* (the special prayer a Jew says before death), Rachel is so focused on the words that she has blocked out the loud blasts from the bombing. She doesn't feel the earth shaking.

Suddenly, springing up from the deepest recesses of her mind, a vista of otherwise random and disjointed memories and impressions erupts to the surface, enveloping her consciousness as she recites the *Shema...*

Rachel is walking to the well with Father. He carries two water pails connected by a wooden bar over his shoulders. Five trips to and from the well will give the family enough water to last from Sunday to Friday. There are two wells: the main well and the "Jewish well." The main well has two large wheels to help bring up the water quickly and easily. It is located in the non-Jewish section Ludmir. The Jewish well is in the Jewish section. It is small and requires vigorous hand pumping to bring up water.

It is Sunday morning, and like most Sunday mornings everything is eerily quiet very early, before dawn.

"Shhh," Father tells Rachel.

He usually doesn't take her with him to get water, but he offered and she was thrilled just accept and spend time with him. They don't talk much; just being with him was what mattered.

~

RACHEL SITS *at the family table with her father. There are a few dozen glass bottles of liquid on the table, each with a thermometer inside. Rachel is cleaning out the inside of one of the bottles with a rag.*

"What do the thermometers do?" she asks Father.

"Good question. If you remember, it took about six weeks for the raisins we bought last February to turn into the wine we used on Passover. Now I'm waiting for the leftover raisin wine to turn into vinegar so I can sell it on the market. When it reaches a certain temperature, then I know it's ready."

"All I know," Rachel says, pinching her nose with her fingers, "is that it smells terrible."

~

*"*RACHEL,*" Father says, "I have a surprise for you. I was going to wait, but I think now is the right time."*

He motions to her to close her eyes and walk over to the kifat, *a type of wooden chest that houses the family tools and other necessities. She closes them — but then slightly opens one eye. He bends over the* kifat *and then turns around to face her. She closes her eye.*

"No peeking," he says.

"No peeking," she replied.

Father opens the chest, his body blocking Rachel's view. She opens her eyes and looks from side to side to try to see, but he successfully shields the object from her view. She sits anxiously awaiting to see what he has. Finally, he pulls it from behind her back.

A doll!

Rachel grabs it with amazement and wonder. "Oh, Father!"

"Do you like it?"

"I love it! It's the best present ever. The best!" She gives the doll a hug. "But where did you get money to pay for it?"

He motions to the bottles on the table. The vinegar.

~

RACHEL *and her family sit around the table, bundled up in winter clothes.*

It is now a couple of years later, after the Polish government issued anti-Semitic decrees targeting and ultimately ruining many Jewish businesses, including Father's. And it was after anti-Semites raided the family's storage shed, stole everything, and left them destitute. It was the terrible winter of 1938–1939, a time of acute desperation.

Rachel rubs her hands together to keep warm. Mist comes out of her mouth as she breaths. She stares at her father and siblings, as cold vapor emerges from their nostrils and quickly evaporates into nothingness.

The entire family is looking at the front door.

And waiting.

Expectantly.

Finally, they hear footsteps. Getting closer. Then the door swings open. A bundled-up visitor swooshes inside, bringing in his wake a swarm of snowflakes, before quickly slamming the door behind him.

The "visitor" is Motl. Underneath his coat, he pulls out a sack. "Didn't I tell you not to worry, that I'd find some?"

He takes the sack and lays it on the table. Then he reaches inside and pulls out...

"A potato!"

"Where'd you find them, Motl?" Rachel asks excitedly.

"Just like I said. Our Polish farmer friends had leftover potatoes and they dumped them in the woods. Since they were so frozen they thought no one would buy them."

"I can't wait any longer," Rachel suddenly says and reaches for a potato in the sack.

"Not so fast, little sister," Motl says. Then, firmly clutching the potato in his hand, he bangs it down on the table. It makes a thud. It is rock-solid frozen!

Rachel's stomach growls so loud that everyone hears it.

"Have no fear," he adds. "Once Hannah cooks them, they'll taste just as delicious as any potatoes."

"How long will it take them to thaw?" Rachel asks, her stomach growling even louder.

"Shouldn't take more than a week, "he replies.

Rachel's face droops. But when the others laugh she realizes he was making a joke; it won't take that long. "Just kidding," Motl adds. "We'll lay them out by the fire and you'll have hot potatoes and potato soup in an hour."

"Oh, Motl," Rachel says, laughing. "You're such a tease."

∾

MOTL BURSTS INTO THE ROOM, breaking Rachel from her reverie. "Father! We have to go!" he shouts. "Our house caught fire!"

Father grabs Rachel with his strong hands and swings her out from under the bed. Then he helps the others out. They run into the street, where the smoke is suffocating and thick. The drone of low-flying planes reverberates everywhere like a swarm of bees. Father grabs Rachel's hand and runs with her across the street. The others follow.

Everywhere, houses are burning. Rushing past several, they finally reach one that isn't. As they stand there, debating for a moment what to do, the door opens. "Come inside, quickly!" the neighbor says.

As she runs inside, Rachel takes one last look at her house. It is engulfed in flames.

~

EVENTUALLY, the bombing stops. An eerie silence descends.

Father looks at the neighbor, and Rachel sees the man nod. Then Father opens the door and steps outside, just to the porch. Rachel is frightened for him. War is outside. She wants her father inside. Safe.

She creeps forward, wanting at least the illusion of safety that being near him always gives her. She hides herself against the wall, so that no one outside — not even Father — can see her. But through the open door, she sees the town burning. Her home is a smoldering ruin. There are giant, smoking craters all over the place.

She can see Father moving forward, his eyes darting about. She wishes so hard that he would just come back inside, that he would hide with her. She wants everything to just go back to how it was.

Wisps of smoke from the bombed-out and still smoking houses lingers in the air. A fog too has settled over the town. It is still quiet… but then Rachel heard something.

Was it a plane? No, this is a different noise. It's coming from some-where in the swirling smoke down the street in the distance. *Father, why are you standing there? Come back inside! Why did you go outside?*

But whatever is making the sound is moving too fast for Father to react. Before he can even take a step, a soldier on a motorcycle emerged from the mist.

Rachel watches the motorcycle stop. Its driver takes off his goggles and says something to Father. She listens intently to pick up any sounds. She speaks an excellent Polish as well as Russian. The language the soldier is speaking, though, is neither. It is German!

Germans soldiers in Ludmir? They aren't supposed to be any. The Russians have a treaty with the Germans. Something is wrong.

Finally, putting his goggles back on, the motorcyclist revs his engine and speed off. Instantly, Father heads back to the house.

As soon as he steps inside, Motl asked, "What happened? What did he say?"

Father shakes his head in a worrisome motion. "Where are the Jews?"

"What did you say?"

"I pretended I didn't understand him, but that's what he said. The Germans are here...and they're looking for Jews."

Even Rachel realizes what this means. Their worst fears have become a reality. This, indeed, was to be a war against the Jews.

CHAPTER 3

MEET THE BLUMS

RACHEL'S FATHER, GERSHON BLUM, HAD COME TO THE UNITED STATES in 1914 and in 1919, staying for about a year each time. He worked long hours in a factory — even ate and slept there — and saved one thousand dollars, which translated into one hundred thousand zlotys, a handsome sum for anyone living in Poland. This allowed him to buy a house in the nice section Ludmir. There was even enough money left over to buy a storefront in the main business district of town.

The Blum house was made of brick and sported a finished wooden floor. Many Jews could not afford anything more than a wooden shack with an earthen floor. Of course, there was no electricity or running water, to say nothing of air- conditioning or heat. In the winter, the oven — relatively primitive because it used wood, not coal — would cook the Blums' food as well as heat up the kitchen and one of the four other rooms of their one-story house. They also had a relatively long dining room table with two chairs, as well as wooden benches. The furniture consisted of a linen closet, a bread closet, a *kifat,* and a shelf for books, mostly volumes of the Torah and other religious writings. This was considered middle class.

Although some of the Jews of Ludmir were doctors and lawyers, most supported themselves by selling various goods, starting with fruits (like strawberries, blueberries, and cherries) and vegetables (like potatoes, onions, beans, and herbs) from the small farms they had. But they also sold animals like chicken, geese, horses, calves, and cows, as well as basic food staples such as eggs, flour, salt, sugar, vinegar, and clothing material like yarn, cotton, and buttons. They would take their wares in wagons to the market and peddle them. Some of the better-off Jews had actual storefronts where they sold groceries.

Father was not wealthy, but he had a store and for a while was able to make a living through it by selling various types of goods. However, in 1935, the Polish authorities promulgated anti-Semitic decrees aimed at the most common Jewish businesses, demanding they upgrade their facilities and pay higher taxes. Both were impossible for Father, and he went out of business. He rented the storefront, but from then on, they had to rely on communal assistance and ingenuity for basic necessities.

For the Sabbath, Father would usually have one of his children bring a large pot to one of the grocers. The grocer would fill it with a few potatoes, some bones, and water — mostly water. The child would bring the pot home and heat it up. Since they rarely had money for wine or flour for challah, the food in the pot was essentially their Sabbath food. As for Sabbath lights, Father would cut a potato in half and stick a candle into each side.

The holidays were no different — cut potatoes for candlesticks; no wine or challah; very little food. However, on Passover, thanks to communal generosity, the Blums had matzah, a little wine, and more food than usual.

One might think that, living under such grueling poverty, their life was depressing. But the Blums were happy. At least, Rachel was. They had a home to live in, and they had each other. What more did one need? And isn't happiness the most important kind of wealth?

From the ages of five to ten, Rachel attended public school until around two o'clock and then a Jewish school for girls from about three to five o'clock, Sunday to Thursday. (Her brothers had attended a full-day Jewish school, *cheder*, until they went out to work, in their teens, as was the norm.) In Rachel's Jewish school, they were taught basic Hebrew, prayers, and Judaism.

Rachel spent much of her free time playing alone under the table in the dining room, amusing herself with a doll she made of a sock (until her father bought her a real doll), or listening to the conversation of the adults sitting around the table. Occasionally, she ventured outside to play, but she was bullied and preferred the indoors.

Although by 1938 the dark clouds of war were already looming, and the Jews knew about it, there was really no place for the Blum family to escape to. Palestine was closed. All of Europe was closed. Their only real choice was to stay in Ludmir and hope for the best.

When the war did come, in 1939, it wasn't so bad. Even after the Germans occupied Poland, they didn't come into Ludmir. In fact, they gave Ludmir to Soviet Russia as part of a truce. The Russians were harsh to the Poles and the Jews in the occupied areas, trying to indoctrinate everyone with Communist ideals and arresting anyone who was wealthier than the Communists liked, and exiling them to Siberia. But the Blums were not affected by that themselves, and the fighting stayed outside of their little town. War was bad, but maybe the family would make it through.

At least that's what they thought... until that dark day in June 1941.

CHAPTER 4

DARKNESS DESCENDS

LUDMIR BURNED FOR DAYS. THE MOTORCYCLIST HAD BEEN AN ADVANCED scout sent by the Germans. It was all part of a surprise attack Hitler called Operation Barbarossa, which began on June 22, 1941.

The Nazi army swept through the shocked Russian army like a sickle through wheat. City after city fell. Ludmir was only twenty miles from the German-Russian treaty line and was one of the first cities bombed.

On June 25 — barely three days after the assault began -- the fires died out and a huge Nazi army drove through. Tanks, trucks, heavy artillery guns, motorcycles, soldiers on foot, all made a deafening racket as they rumbled down the streets of the shattered town.

The Blums hid for a few days with the neighbor who had taken them in. They couldn't stay there forever, though, and with their own home destroyed they moved to Father's store, which he still owned and had been renting out until then. There was nothing left there except a few pieces of broken furniture — everything else had been looted while the town burned — but at least it was a place to stay.

They gradually heard about the casualties that had come from the bombing. So many had died! One large group of almost five hundred Jews who had taken shelter together in a basement had thought they were safe — until the building they were in was hit and started burning uncontrollably. They were not able to get out.

A few days later, the Nazis decreed that all radios and books be turned in. The next day they made a spectacle of burning the books in a bonfire.

The Germans replaced the Russians with a Ukrainian police force, and the new police started randomly hauling Jews in off the streets, hundreds at a time, and bringing them to the town prison. No one knew what happened to the people who were arrested, and none were ever released. Just walking in the streets had become dangerous.

From August to December, a new normal settled over Ludmir. Mass kidnappings happened often, and everyone understood that the police were killing most of those people. It was impossible to ignore the mass graves that were appearing and growing in the prison courtyard.

THE GERMANS SET up a Jewish council, called the Judenrat, which was to serve as a liaison between the Jewish community and the Nazi rulers. Many Jews were originally encouraged by this, as it seemed like a system of government was being put in place. Surely the Germans wouldn't set up something like that if they were just going to kill everyone.

One of the people appointed to the Judenrat was Mr. Dov Stitzer, Gershon Blum's brother-in-law, whom the family lovingly called "Uncle." He helped the Blums wherever he could, even giving Father a job in the Judenrat itself. It was menial work, but it was better than most jobs, and the workers were given lunch, albeit not a very substantial one. Furthermore, Uncle Dov helped Rachel's eldest brothers, Wolf and Motl, get work in a mill he owned before the war and which the Nazis allowed him to continue to operate. It helped a little bit with the hunger, but only a little. Unrelenting hunger was becoming a regular fact of life.

Even though the Judenrat gave the Jews a sense of hope, the reality was that it was just a vehicle in the Nazi's diabolical scheme of deception to further the Final Solution, the extermination of the entire Jewish people. It was through the various Judenrats that Nazi decrees, either through forceful coercion or false assurances, were carried out.

One of those decrees was that Jews over the age of ten had to wear two yellow badges: one over the front and the other on the back. Any Jew caught without the star risked beating, imprisonment, or execution. This helped the Nazis identify Jews in preparation for their ultimate aim, which was to deport and exterminate them all.

The Judenrat also oversaw the distribution of bread tickets. However, Jews were allotted only about two pounds of bread per week, not enough to live on.

As their choices narrowed, their hunger grew.

CHAPTER 5

THE YOUNG SMUGGLER

"No," Rachel insisted more strongly than she believed she was capable of. "I won't do it!" She had never disobeyed Father before, and certainly never raised her voice, but this was going too far.

"You're our best chance, Rachel," Father said, motioning with his eyes to her brothers who were in the room.

"No. You know better than anyone how dangerous it is."

"It's dangerous if we do nothing. Do you see how pale and gaunt Simcha is?"

Rachel had noticed. "But why not send Motl or Wolf?"

"They speak with a Jewish accent."

"So do I."

"Your Polish is perfect. You went to public school. They didn't."

"But they'll know I'm Jewish."

"No they won't. They'll think you're just a Polish girl looking to exchange some buttons" — he jiggled a small sack — "for bread."

"But they'll know."

"How will they know?"

"Because I am."

"Not if you don't tell them."

"But they'll know anyway."

"How?"

"Because I'm scared." Rachel paused. Her father didn't seem to have an answer for that. "If I'm scared they'll know something is wrong and they'll figure out that I'm Jewish and they'll turn me in."

Father sat down on a bench and asked Rachel to sit down next to him. He then clasped her hand and held it warmly in his. "I know you're scared, Rachel. We all are. I'm scared too." She looked at him. He continued, "But you can find it in you not to be scared. You can. You're much stronger than you think."

"No I'm not."

Father paused and took a long look at his daughter, weighing if he should tell her what was really on his mind. Finally, he pursed his lips and explained, "You know how you always ask me about your mother, what she was like?"

"Yes, and you usually avoid telling me anything."

"Well, let me tell you now." Father held Rachel's hand even more firmly. "She suffered a lot. That's why I never told you much about her. We had a very tough life together. The war. Even before the war, I spent time in the United States to save money. She suffered, but she was the strong one. She was the one who gave me strength. No matter how bad things were, she had this amazing attitude that somehow things would work out for the best. No — it was even more than that. Nothing was bad. Somehow, no matter how much we suffered, nothing was bad. I don't know how she did it, but that's what she always said. That's what she believed, and that's the way she lived her life — no matter what was going on."

A tear formed in Rachel's eye. "But I'm not her."

Father let go of Rachel's hand and scratched his head. Then he stood up and paced back and forth while Rachel just sat there, trying to control her tears.

"I mean I don't even know where to go," she said. "I don't even know how to get past the Ukrainian guards."

"That's not so hard," Father responded. "Motl has been watching them. There are a couple of places, behind some houses, that are more isolated than others. They come and go at regular intervals. He's pretty sure —"

"I can't do it, Father. I can't. I'm sorry, but I can't."

"You're right," Father finally conceded. "You're right, of course. I shouldn't have asked you. It was wrong of me."

"It's not that I don't want to help."

"Of course not. I know that if you thought you could help you would. You're a good girl."

A lump formed in Rachel's throat. She had a hard time swallowing. "I am a good girl."

"You are. And I know you are."

"I'm just scared."

"You have every right to be."

At this point, Motl spoke up. "Father, she's right. You can't force her. I'll go."

"No, you can't. None of you boys can. The second you open your mouth they'll know you're Jewish. You can't hide that."

"I can," Motl insisted.

As Rachel watched them speak, their voices faded into the distance. All she could focus on was her brother Simcha, lying on the couch, so weak already. Motl and Wolf at least could join a labor group and receive food, however meager the portions. Simcha wouldn't last a day on a labor detail. He was completely dependent on food being brought to him.

By this time, Father and Motl had raised their voices so much that they were yelling at each other.

"You can't go," Father shouted.

"We have no choice!" Motl shouted back.

"No, my word is final!"

"I'll go myself!"

Then, in middle of the shouting, a small, quiet voice was heard.

"I'll go."

Father and Motl didn't even hear it. They continued arguing.

Then Rachel said it again. "I'll go."

Father and Motl stopped talking.

"I'll go," Rachel repeated a third time. Father looked at her and took a seat next to her. "Give me the buttons," she said.

"But, Rachel, you were right," Father said, clasping her hand again. "If they sense you're afraid, they'll figure out that something is wrong."

"Then I guess I'll just have to not be afraid," she replied.

THE STARS WERE out and it was dark outside. Father, Hannah, Motl, Wolf, and Simcha sat inside the front room of the storefront.

"She should've been back already," Motl said to his father, who stood up and paced back and forth.

"Don't you think I know that!" he snapped.

"I'll go look for her," Motl said.

"No. It's my responsibility."

"Father," Motl insisted, "I've been watching the guards. I know their movements."

"There are more guards and they're more on the lookout at night."

"Doesn't matter. I know what to do."

"Where will you even go to look for her? You can't go."

"If it's too dangerous for me, it's even more dangerous for you. Father, I'll go."

"I shouldn't have let her go," Father repeated.

"She agreed. She wanted to. You heard the conviction in her voice."

"I still shouldn't have let her go. I'm her father. How could I even suggest it? Oh, God, why did You put me in such a situation?"

Suddenly, the front door swung open. Out of the dark emerged the little figure of Rachel, carrying a sack of something.

Immediately, Father ran over and hugged her. So did Motl and Wolf. Even Simcha got up from his daze to greet her.

They led her to the back room and she spilled the contents on the table. Two big loaves of bread, three long carrots, four potatoes. A veritable feast.

"The buttons worked good," she told them, "but I think I can do better next time with socks or stockings. Or even some cotton. Can you get some for me?"

They looked at her, stunned.

"What are you looking at?" she asked.

"My little girl," Father said, "is not a little girl anymore."

"What do you mean?"

"Nothing. Listen, I thought about it and I don't want you to go out smuggling food for us again. It's too dangerous. We'll figure something else out."

"What are you talking about? I'm the best one to do this. I'm the only one who can do this in the family. Plus, I figured out some things. You know the place behind the house near the woods? I think it's an even better place for me to sneak out. Plus —"

"Tell us about it later, Rachel. Now let's warm this up and make some dinner."

CHAPTER 6

IVAN AND MARIA

IVAN ROLUK MARVELED HOW THE SCENERY HAD CHANGED SO QUICKLY. A moment ago, his train was rattling along the tracks through a thick funnel of tall green pine trees. and now it emerged in a barren, charred field.

He pulled the train to a stop. The steam engine let out an exasperated hiss.

Immediately, the peace and quiet was shattered by the sounds of German soldiers running about and barking orders. He watched as dozens of soldiers carried fellow wounded soldiers on stretchers to the empty cars behind the engine.

Ivan took out a cigarette.

It reminded him of his early days in Moscow shortly after the Communist Revolution in 1917. Maria, his wife, worked as a nurse in the Kremlin for none other than the great Communist leader Vladimir Ilyich Lenin. It was a day similar to this: a deceptively blue sky, the sweet smell of spring in the air, flowers blossoming.

And death all about.

As he took a long puff from his cigarette, the image of those days flowed into his mind.

Soldiers disembarked from a train, shouting orders in Russian. Wounded comrades were removed from stretchers. Doctors and nurses, like Maria, performed quick examinations and directed the wounded toward preassigned areas.

Then there was an explosion...and gunshots.

Ivan watched with horror from the train as smoke enveloped the area where he had last seen Maria. Oh G-d, no.

He ran in the direction he had last seen her, terrified what he might find. Many of the wounded on the stretchers were now dead. Bullets were whizzing by, but he didn't care. All that mattered was Maria. What was his life without her?

Then he saw it — the white uniform of a nurse face down on the ground. His heart sank...

Behind him he heard a familiar voice. "Ivan."

It was Maria. She emerged from the smoke, coughing, her white dress dirtied — but she was alive.

After that close call, Ivan and Maria Roluk decided to leave Moscow. It wasn't clear which side would win, Lenin's Red Army or the anti-Communist White Army. Either way, it was extremely dangerous to be so close to the action. As a machinist (the name they called people who knew about trains), Ivan would be able to find work easily enough. But even if he couldn't, he and Maria decided to settle as far away as they could. That's what brought them to Ludmir, in the Ukraine.

Now, here they were many years later, transplanted Russians living among Ukrainians conscripted by the Germans.

Ivan watched the Germans load wounded soldiers onto the train. He had no love for the Germans, but as long as they valued his expertise he felt relatively safe. The truth was that he was no fan of the Communists either. He had seen what they could do. Of course, the Nazis were worse, especially when it came to the Jews. But it mattered less to him who won the war — the Germans or the Russians — than that he, his wife, and their son were safe. And they were, as long as he did his job, which is exactly what he planned to do. If he was lucky they just might make it through the war alive.

CHAPTER 7

THE RUSSIAN SOLDIERS

ALMOST AS SOON AS THE NAZIS TOOK OVER LUDMIR, THEY CONSCRIPTED Jews for labor. Even young Rachel was put on a work detail. They sent her to the fields to uproot weeds.

Often Rachel snuck away from her work and wandered around or even fell asleep on the ground in the forest.

One day she wandered near the old army barracks that had housed the Polish soldiers until 1939 when the Russians took over and moved in. Those very same barracks were now used as a prison for the Russian soldiers captured by the Nazis.

During one of her walks Rachel noticed the Russians, under armed guard, digging a ditch. The next day she returned and saw them digging again. *That's strange. Why are the Germans making the Russians dig so much?*

Day after day she came back and observed how the ditch was becoming wider and longer.

Jews were doing plenty of digging too. Often Rachel saw Jewish slave laborers consisting of twenty or thirty men coming and going through the ghetto entrance. Invariably, they were led by some Ukrainian soldiers, with one German soldier directing them.

One sunny day, as usual, Rachel slipped away from her work in the field and headed toward the woods. Just as she was about to enter the woods she heard a voice shout, "Stop!"

Not hesitating a moment to turn around, she darted into the thick forest of trees as fast as she could.

After what seemed like an interminable amount of time she finally stopped running and leaned up against a tree, huffing and puffing. As her breathing relaxed, she heard some shouting in the distance.

Curious, staying under the cover of the woods, she crept toward the source of the sound. She crouched behind a bush at the edge of the forest and watched as German guards led a contingent of bedraggled Russian soldiers toward another group of Russian soldiers.

Suddenly — machine gun fire!

Aghast, Rachel covered her eyes. The machine gun fire continued. She put her hands over her ears, but it was a futile attempt to block out the horror.

Finally, she got up the strength to stand on her feet and run. She ran and ran and ran...

She emerged from the woods at the edge of the Jewish section and continued running. Her heart was racing as she dashed across a street, down a few back allies, past some labor battalions, and then into the store. Running into her father's arms, she started sobbing.

"My child, calm down. What's the matter?"

"I... I... I saw it... with my own eyes."

"Shh, shh. Saw what?"

Through her sobs, Rachel blurted out, "The Germans... the Russian soldiers. Then they... they... the Germans... they fired their guns... again and again... and the Russians were just falling down... into..."

Her father gently stroked her hair. "It's okay, my child. It's okay."

Rachel couldn't speak. Tears were streaming down her face. She breathed rapidly, almost to the point of hyperventilating.

"Shh," Father said in a soothing tone. He held her close and repeated, "Shh... shh."

Finally, Rachel's breathing slowed and normalized. "Father," she blurted, "will they do that to us?"

Patting her with vigor he answered, "No, my child. No." Luckily, Rachel could not see her father's eyes, which were filled with worry.

CHAPTER 8

STEPHAN JOINS THE SS

MARIA AND IVAN ROLUK WERE BOTH PROUD OF THEIR SON, STEPHAN... and worried. They had raised him well. He was kindhearted and soft spoken. He knew good from bad and avoided peers who were troublemakers. He even avoided the heavy drinking that so many Poles, Ukrainians, and transplanted Russian youth indulged in.

However, in the crazy, topsy-turvy, upside down world of Europe in 1941, fifteen-year-old Stephan Roluk could not avoid the Nazis, and the choice was either to be their victim or their helper. When the local SS chief suggested to Ivan that his son "volunteer" in the local SS office, it was an offer one could not refuse. And, after all, it was only paperwork. Stephan had nothing to do with any of the *aktions*, roundup activities and atrocities that the SS was notorious for. Stephan was conscripted much like his father into the service of the Nazis. He was more than qualified for the office work they assigned him, and it was, for the time being, a way of surviving.

But Maria and Ivan were worried. They were worried for Stephan's safety — and for his soul. If you hung around bad people long enough you would begin to think and be like them. Yet, there was really no choice in the matter — not for Stephan and not for Maria and Ivan.

CHAPTER 9

BABI YAR

IT WAS A DARK, MOONLESS NIGHT. TWO UKRAINIAN GUARDS IN UNIFORM walked past a house on the outskirts of Ludmir, not far from the woods. After they passed, a little girl emerged from the woods and snuck unnoticed past the spot they had occupied just moments before.

She was obviously carrying something under her blouse, which was bulging. She looked left. Then right. Then darted across the street.

She came to a door, opened it, and slipped inside into the store-front. She gingerly opened the door at the back of the store. Her family was sitting on the floor, huddled together. There was no furniture in the bare room.

"Rachel's back," Hannah announced. She was the first to greet Rachel and help her take out the hidden stash under her clothes. It was a large loaf of bread and a few potatoes. The others gathered around to view the day's "catch."

"That's my girl," Father said lovingly, patting his daughter on the head. He took the bread and distributed portions. Hannah took the potatoes and put them in a pot on a makeshift stove of rocks. She started a fire underneath. Rachel squatted down next to her to help.

Father and the boys sat on the floor to eat their meager but much-appreciated portions. Wolf announced, "I heard people saying they're going to make two ghettos."

"What does that mean?" Motl asked.

"They're going to cram all the Jews into the smaller ghetto," Wolf replied, "on the other side of the non-Jewish part of town. This side, even though it's larger, will be forbidden."

"Wolf," Father said sternly, "stop scaring people with rumors, empty rumors. Anyway, what are you complaining about? As long as your uncle is on the Jewish Council, he'll continue to get us jobs and look out for us. Hannah, how is it going with the children?"

"It's so heartbreaking. They're just newborns. They don't know that their parents are dead or in hiding. But at least they're alive. What's going to be with them after the war, I don't know."

"The war will be over one day," her father reassured her, "and they'll be returned to their parents."

"Be realistic," Wolf interjected. "They're never going to be returned to their parents."

"Don't talk that way, Wolf. Besides, Hannah knows which children were sent to which non-Jewish homes. After the war, thanks to Hannah, they'll be reunited with their parents, or at least with their relatives. She'll make sure they're returned."

"Father, don't you see? Don't you know what's going on?"

"I'm not naive, my son."

"Yeah, but do you know what's really going on?"

"Tell us, Wolf," Motl said. "Tell us what's going on."

"Well, I heard from someone. Remember those thirty boys they sent to Kiev."

"Yes," Motl asserted. "To lay underground telephone lines, just like they did here."

Wolf shook his head. "That's not what they did, they…"

"Wolf!" Father said, raising his voice. "Enough of this talk."

"It's true."

"What did you hear?" Motl asked.

"They took Jews — thousands and thousands of them. Some say thirty thousand. To a place called Babi Yar —"

"Wolf, no more talk of this," Father said. "Hannah, how are those potatoes coming?"

CHAPTER 10

MARIA'S GREAT FEAR

MARIA ROLUK HAD AN ARISTOCRATIC AIR ABOUT HER. SHE DID NOT dress like a peasant. She wore boots with laces, which was very stylish for those days. When she and her husband, Ivan, escaped Moscow in 1917, they took some money out with them and bought a house in Ludmir, as well as about two acres of land for farming. It was not uncommon for people to own a house as well as a small parcel of land on the outskirts. The Roluks lived off the land, like most people of Ludmir, and on the wages Ivan received from the Germans for his services.

During the winter months, when it was too cold to venture outside, there was not much for Maria to do. After she would tend the couple of animals in their barn, she passed the time by knitting, using wool from the fur of some Angora rabbits she kept.

Other than that, she would socialize with the other women; though not much of a gossiper, she was keen to hear stories about Nazi atrocities. She had seen them mistreat Jews, and was well aware that they had rounded them up and locked them in a ghetto. But she was more worried about the stories of what happened to the local non-Jews, especially those who had been accused of helping and hiding Jews. The SS would come and arrest them, usually never to be seen or heard from again.

A recent rash of these arrests, or worse, put everyone on edge more than ever. Maria's fear eventually subsided a little, but the cold Ukrainian winter was a good excuse to stay at home and knit. It was a calming way to pass the time.

CHAPTER 11

A DECREE FROM BERLIN

THE YEAR 1941 TURNED INTO 1942. JEWISH LIVES BECAME EVEN cheaper. Every day, Jews were kidnapped or conscripted into labor battalions and sent east. Most were never heard from again.

One morning, as Rachel was sitting in the shop with the rest of her family, a truck with a loudspeaker made its way up and down the battered Jewish section. "Tomorrow morning at nine o'clock, all Jews must assemble at the central synagogue. Anyone who fails to do so will face severe consequences. Tomorrow morning at nine o'clock, all Jews must assemble." With no other choice, the Jews complied.

At the assembly, a Nazi announced that Jews were to be restricted to a certain area inside Ludmir. Everyone outside that designated area had to move in. Jews living on farms or in houses on the outskirts of town also had to move in.

In the Judenrat office the next day, Uncle Dov said to Father, "Some are escaping to the forest to join the partisans. Have you considered it?"

"I think the best place is here, certainly as long as you're on the Judenrat."

"Don't fool yourself, Gershon. No one is safe. No one. Why not join those who are fleeing into the forest?"

"I have children. How will they survive? Besides, aren't we serving the Germans a purpose? Aren't we their labor force?"

"As long as we serve their needs, they'll let us live. But who knows how long that will be. No one is safe. Think about joining the partisans."

"In the forest? With my family? Not possible."

It was a dilemma Jews throughout Europe faced. What could they do? Where could they go? For tight-knit Jewish families like the Blums, there was really no choice.

~

SHORTLY AFTER PASSOVER 1942, Father and Uncle Dov observed workers sinking lumber poles into the ground. "What are they doing?" Father asked.

"It's a fence. Soon we'll be locked in completely."

Indeed, by May 1942 the barbwire fence was completed. If a plane flew over Ludmir, it would see the town divided into three parts: a non-Jewish section between the two Jewish ghettos, each surrounded by barbed wire fences.

The non-Jewish section was distinguished by a magnificent, undamaged parliamentary building occupied by the Germans, a serene park, and a beautiful, relatively new three-story school, with Nazi flags outside signifying their headquarters.

The Jewish section consisted of Ludmir's two ghettos: a large one and a small one. The small ghetto, which was a residential neighborhood before the war, was crammed with Jews. Its houses were mostly one story high and wooden, although a few were brick and two stories high.

Although most Jews resided in the smaller ghetto, the Blums' storefront was in the larger one, where there were relatively few people. There were other stores along the same street as the Blums' store, but none of them were active.

~

ONE DAY, as Rachel gazed out the storefront window, she saw her uncle walking erratically down the street. He looked very disoriented. Motl also noticed and called to the back room, "Father, come."

"What?"

Motl pointed to outside. Father saw Uncle Dov walking this way and that way, completely disoriented. "Dov," Father called as he opened the front door.

Uncle Dov did not notice. Father called his name a second time, but again he seemed oblivious. Finally, Father ventured outside and strode toward Uncle Dov. Only when he got near him did he realize how pale he looked. "What's the matter? Father asked.

"A decree," Uncle Dov replied.

"A decree?"

"From Berlin."

"Explain."

"Seven hundred people, Gershon. Seven hundred!"

"What are you talking about?"

"That's what they said. It's a decree."

"A decree for what?"

"We must hand over seven hundred... seven hundred people. The elderly and children."

"For what purpose?"

His hands trembling, his voice quavering, Uncle Dov finally blurted out, "Extermination. It's a decree. From Berlin."

Father put his hands over his mouth.

"They say there's no averting it," Uncle Dov added.

"Oh, my God!"

"I don't know what to do. How can we give them a list?"

"What about a bribe?"

"We've been collecting gold, watches, and other and giving them to the Germans as bribes since the beginning. Even if we could find more and even if it helped to delay them a little... it would only delay the inevitable." Dov grabbed Father firmly by his shirt collar. "Don't you get it? They won't stop at these seven hundred. Next time it'll be seven thousand. And after that everyone."

"Oh, my God!"

"Gershon," Uncle Dov added, "you know that earlier this month they conscripted one hundred Jews to dig three large pits about six miles from here, in Piyatidne."

"Yes. I heard about it. The pits are for an underground storage bunker and some sort of airplane hangar."

"Gershon, now they've asked us to send them one thousand Jews to dig three pits. Huge pits... it's not for storage. It's for us."

Father saw that Uncle Dov was absolutely serious. Suddenly, a wave of terror flowed through him. He looked back at the store and his children. Then he turned back toward Dov. "What... what can we do?"

"Have you thought about building a hiding place?"

"Yes, for the longest time. I've had an idea, but I need wood, a lot of it."

"I can get you that."

~

THE NEXT DAY, four wagons of lumber pulled up in front of the Blums' storefront.

The plan was to create a false ceiling in the back room. And, indeed, in almost miraculously quick fashion, the Blums built the hideout. Without ladders or even nails, they somehow finished the job in a day.

The immediate problem was that the wood on the ceiling looked brand-new, while the walls and the rest of the room appeared old. It was obvious that there was a freshly built hiding place up in the ceiling.

Father decided to collect newspapers, twigs, and other flammable items. He then started a fire inside the room, which quickly filled with smoke. After a while, he put out the fire. Now the ceiling looked old, as if it had been there for years.

The hiding place would save their lives.

CHAPTER 12

ASSIGNMENT: TREBLINKA

It was a special assignment, the SS man told Ivan Roluk. He would take a train of wounded soldiers all the way to Warsaw.

Ivan had never been asked to take a train to Warsaw. At most, he had taken wounded Germans to Lublin.

"In Warsaw," the SS man told him coldly, "you'll receive further instructions. Special instructions."

Ivan looked at him.

"Don't worry," the SS man said with a sly smile. "You'll be back here in no time. You're too valuable to us here."

Ivan didn't show it on the outside, but inside he let out a big sigh of relief. "What type of special assignment?" he asked.

The SS man erupted in a huge laugh. "Do you want to get me sent to the front?"

Ivan tried to make his lips eke out a smile. "I didn't mean anything by the question. I was just asking."

The Nazi pulled a cigarette out of his pocket and lit it. He took a long puff and then took an even longer look at Ivan. Ivan stood there stoically, not sure how to react.

"I'll tell you this, Roluk," the SS man finally said. "It has to do with Jews. We're transporting them from Warsaw to work camps in the east."

"The east?"

The Nazi took another puff. "Don't worry, Roluk. Not too far east. If we're lucky they'll only ask you to make one run and then send you back to continue your work here with us." Ivan looked at him, trying not to give away the fear in his heart.

"I mean it, Roluk. There's nothing to worry about. You'll be back home with your family the next day."

The Nazi took one more puff and then threw the cigarette on the ground, stamping on it with his perfectly shined black boot. "You'll see. It's just a few hours east of Warsaw. A place you probably never heard of. Treblinka."

CHAPTER 13

THE WARNING

August 31, 1942

LATE AFTERNOON. THE SUN WAS LOW OVER THE UKRAINIAN FOREST. A Ukrainian guard in uniform with a gun over his shoulder walked inside a section of the barbwire fence on the outskirts of the Jewish ghetto not far from the woods. After he passed, Rachel emerged from the woods and squeezed under a part of the barbwire. It was a tiny crawl space that only someone her size could fit through.

She walked into her family's store to the sound of arguing. "The bribe worked," Father told the others.

"I don't believe that's the reason," Wolf said.

"Did they take away the seven hundred Jews?"

"No, but it's for some other reason."

"What?"

"Something bigger. Something worse."

Suddenly they noticed Rachel. Wolf looked at her empty hands and the disappointed look on her face. "Nothing again?" he asked.

Rachel shook her head.

"I'm hungry," Simcha groaned in a pathetic voice.

"What are we going to do?" Wolf asked.

There was a knock at the door. It was Uncle Dov. He had an ashen look on his face. He took a long, hard look at each member of the family. There were tears in his eyes. Father tried to escort him out of the room, but Uncle Dov did not let him. "No, everyone has to hear this." They gathered around and noticed his hands shaking almost uncontrollably. "Tomorrow... tomorrow morning, before dawn, there will be an *aktion*."

"What's an *aktion*?" Rachel asked.

"A round-up. They're going to assemble all the Jews... and lead everyone to Piyatidne." Silence. No one could speak. "Listen to me," Uncle Dov said sternly. "Don't wait for dawn. Clean up your place *now*. Make it look like no one has been living here. Then go up into your hiding place. All of you. There's no time to delay."

They were too stunned to move.

Uncle Dov saw their paralysis and shouted, "Now! I must go and prepare my family. Quick! There's no time."

CHAPTER 14

THE BRUTAL TRUTH

IVAN ROLUK COULDN'T BELIEVE HIS EYES. HE THOUGHT HE HAD SEEN everything. After all, he'd been driving to the front and picking up wounded soldiers. He'd seen more blood and gore than most. But this was not just blood and gore. This was...there were no words to describe it.

What was this place?

The sign along the tracks read *Treblinka.*

He knew things were bad the day before, when he pulled his long train of empty cars — empty cattle cars — into the Warsaw station. He had seen thousands of people, Jews, lined up in the plaza, the *Umschlagplatz,* with their suitcases and earthly belongings in hand.

Did they know where they were going, what was about to happen to them? Probably not. Like him, they were told that the trains were to transport them to the east — to camps where they would be put to work. Forced labor was horrible. But this was war. War was horrible.

However, as he pulled out of the station hours later with his load of perhaps five thousand Jews, he knew something didn't make sense. First, they were squeezed into the cattle cars so tightly that it was beyond inhumane. Second, they were not given food or even water. Third, many -- maybe most — of the passengers were elderly men and women, as well as little children. What type of workers could they possibly make? How productive could they be?

Then one of the SS officers joined him up front, making the coarsest remarks about the Jews. Ivan, for his part, didn't have contact with many Jews. He knew a few, but only a few, and did not particularly like or dislike them. He figured there were some bad ones as well as some good ones, like everyone else. While Ivan felt a little uncomfortable with the SS officer's barrage of curses against the Jews, he was not about to say anything or let on that he thought it was too much. But then the fellow said something else.

"And the best part is," the Nazi said, "these stupid Jews think they're going to a work camp, a regular family outing -- as if we really need old Jews and little children working for us. Ha!"

Ivan wanted to ask, *If you're not transporting them to work, what are you transporting them for? And what is this place called Treblinka?* But he dared not ask.

However, now as his train pulled to a stop at the Treblinka station, he was beginning to understand. The truth was slowly dawning on him.

Then in the distance he saw a thick column of black smoke, and for the first time he knew. He knew how truly evil the Nazis were. Treblinka was not a work camp. It was not a place where people labored under brutal conditions.

Treblinka was a death camp.

The Jews were not there to perform labor. They were there to be murdered *en masse*, away from the eyes of others.

CHAPTER 15

THE FINAL SOLUTION

September 1, 1942.

DAWN.

Rachel and her family hid in the ceiling, shivering with fear, cramped in a small area where all they could do was lie flat on their stomachs.

There was a loud rap on the front door. Then another. And another.

Finally, a crash.

Two Nazi soldiers, along with four husky Ukrainian thugs, smashed the large glass window of the storefront. Once inside, they made their way over the shattered shards to the door leading to the back room where Rachel and her family were hiding.

Up in the ceiling hideout, all the Blums were terror stricken. They heard another crashing sound. Then they heard the door being hacked open with an ax. In seconds, they heard the door fall to the floor with a loud thud.

There was yelling... shouting... in German and Ukrainian.

"All Jews out! All Jews out!"

Hiding just a few feet above the shouting murderers, they dared not breathe.

"Jews out! Jews out!"

Rachel was afraid to even twitch.

The intruders could be heard rumbling below, shouting and cursing.

Finally, after what seemed like an eternity, they left. There was dead silence for a few long moments. In the wake of the quietness, Rachel could clearly hear the not-so-distant sounds outside all around: trucks, gunfire.

Ludmir was in chaos.

In a scene reminiscent of the turmoil that had been taking place all over Nazi-occupied Europe, the Jews of Ludmir were rounded up — men and women, elderly and children. In lines of five to eight abreast, the crowd stretched as far as the eye could see. Everybody pressed tightly together, united in suffering. Side by side they marched. Gnarled, elderly Jews alongside young, erect workers, intellectuals, and simple folk. They marched — a veritable army of women and children, the ill and the weak — all completely helpless.

The sky was clear blue, not a cloud in sight. It was a perfect day. Nature at its best. The Earth was in full bloom. The sun poured down its bountiful rays and bathed the world in a golden glow. But beneath the serene, beautiful aquamarine skies, the hapless Jewish victims marched inexorably toward their final destination, Piyatidne.

From that day for the next two weeks, the Nazis — with the help of the Ukrainians — massacred Ludmir's Jews. According to estimates, about 18,000 were slaughtered.

Some Jews being led to Piyatidne attempted to escape. Most of them were caught and taken to the prison, and from there to the killing fields of Piyatidne. The walls of the jail were covered in writing, *Avenge the Jewish blood that has been spilled!*

During this entire time, Rachel and her family hid in the attic, never once coming down.

LIKE MANY PLACES IN EUROPE, Ludmir had a rich Jewish history, serving as home to a Jewish community since at least the 1200s.

In the 1800s, Ludmir was also the hometown of the "Maiden of Ludmir," Channah Rachel Verbermacher. Although the facts of her story are shrouded in mystery, she was known as a wonder-working woman who attracted several followers. Women and men alike would come to her for prayers and advice, which she would freely share modestly from behind a curtain.

World War I devastated Ludmir, like it did countless Jewish towns in Eastern Europe. Retreating Russian troops set part of the town on fire and committed random acts of bloodshed.

After World War I, Ludmir officially became part of the newly recreated Poland. It was a time of relative prosperity. However, it was also a time of ideological confusion, and many Jewish youths embraced ideologies foreign to and even in open opposition to traditional Jewish values.

By the 1930s, most Ludmir's inhabitants were Jews, about 22,000 at the time of the war. Most lived apart from the non-Jews, in a Jewish section, with many of the Jews running small farms on the outskirts of town.

But now, less than two weeks before the Day of Judgment 1942 (September 12), the rich Jewish life of Ludmir had become nothing more than a memory.

CHAPTER 16

TREBLINKA!

MARIA ROLUK HAD NEVER SEEN HER HUSBAND SO DISTRAUGHT. SHE hadn't seen him drink like this in twenty years. But now he was asking for yet another glass of vodka.

All he kept saying was a strange word she had never heard: "Treblinka."

And all she kept on asking was, "What is Treblinka?"

All he answered, if he answered anything, was, "Treblinka."

Then the front door opened and Stephan walked in. Ivan looked at his son in the SS uniform and stared at him as he made his way over to the table. Ivan tracked every step with his eyes, which seemed to be on fire. Without warning, he jumped out of his chair, shouted "Treblinka!" and raced toward Stephan like a madman, grabbing him fiercely by the collar, and droving him back into the far wall.

"Stop!" Maria shouted.

Ivan looked deep into his son's eyes, a look that could kill. Stephan had never seen his father like this. He smelled the vodka on his breath. He didn't know how to react, and even if he wanted to react there was nothing he could do, his father's grip was so powerful.

After what seemed like an eternity, Ivan released his son, spit on the floor next to him, and muttered, "Treblinka." Then he fell to the floor and started crying like a baby.

CHAPTER 17

A DEAFENING QUIET

As the mass murder of Ludmir's Jews at Piyatidne continued, Rachel and her family remained up in the attic. They dared not leave. They dared not move.

The attic was incredibly cramped. There was no room to even sit up. Each person went in headfirst with hands stretched in front. The way they went in was the way they stayed there.

There was no food. No water. No bathroom. Day after day the Blums heard the sounds of horror emanating from the outside: shouting, screaming, gunfire.

And then one day it stopped. There was an eerie quiet. You notice the sudden disappearance of 18,000 people in a small town. The quiet was deafening.

Father was the first one to venture out. One by one, he helped his children down from the ceiling. First Hannah. Then Motl. Then Wolf. Then Simcha. And finally, Rachel.

Rachel, though, was so close to death that her tongue stuck to her palate (one of the signs of imminent death by starvation). She couldn't even muster the energy to wet her tongue. Her world was spinning around. She couldn't move.

Her father briefly left the store to survey the situation. Later, he returned with a little water. At first, Rachel couldn't even take a sip. They wet her lips, but still she couldn't move her tongue. Finally, she swallowed a drop of water they had put on her lips. Then she took a small sip. Then another sip. Then she sat up. Soon enough she could walk.

DURING THE DAY, Rachel and her family went back up to the attic and stayed hidden. They only came out at night -- not to go anywhere or do anything, but just to stretch and look for a little food.

The Nazis had created two ghettos. The Blums were hiding in a part of the ghetto that had now been declared off limits. The Jews themselves called that area the "Death Ghetto" (*Toiteh Ghetto* in Yiddish), because anyone living there was illegal and those caught would be killed. The other half of the ghetto, which was physically smaller, where Jews could live if they had working papers, was called the "Living Ghetto" (*Leibedik Ghetto* in Yiddish).

ONE NIGHT IN NOVEMBER 1942, Rachel's brother Motl went out at night in search of food and found a loaf of bread. On his way back he went stealthily from building to building because Ukrainian guards lurked about. He would go behind or in one building, listen for any sounds, look around, and then go to the next building. He was in the building just across from the Blums' store when he suddenly heard footsteps. He stood perfectly still until the sound of the footsteps died down. He waited. And waited.

Still not quite sure it was safe, he left the loaf where he was and made his way out, toward the building where his family was hiding up in the ceiling. It was so quiet that even the smallest sound was magnified. However, he made it into the storefront without getting caught. He let out a big — but quiet — sigh of relief.

As he was about to climb up to the hiding place, he heard the footsteps again. They were unmistakable and coming closer. Motl had no chance to do anything.

"Stop!" a man said in Ukrainian. Rachel and her family heard everything as they hid in the ceiling just a couple of feet from where the Ukrainian had found Motl. He pointed his gun at Motl and told him to come with him.

The next night the Blums found the loaf of bread in the building next to theirs. Motl had probably dropped it there to help his family remain hidden, because if his captors had seen the loaf they might have suspected it was for others. Or if they came back and found the loaf in the other building they would have intensified their search there rather than anywhere else. In either event, as noble as he was to the end, Motl was murdered by the Nazis.

~

ALTHOUGH THE BLUMS were hiding up in the ceiling at night, the frigid winter wind would whip through the storefront below. The windows and doors were never repaired. Even up in the ceiling the freezing cold was unbearable.

In early December, on a particularly cold night, Simcha, the youngest brother, froze to death in the ceiling. He was a quiet, unassuming teenager who never hurt anyone.

The family didn't know what to do with the body. There was no place to bury him and if they took his body out of the ceiling and left it on the ground, it would raise suspicions that others were hiding in the vicinity. So they kept his body up in the ceiling, even as they themselves went into the hiding place each day. After a week, however, the smell of the decaying body was so great that they had no choice but to remove it. There was no place to leave it except in the store and cover it up with rags.

Unfortunately, the Nazis and their Ukrainian henchmen were on the alert for any sign of Jews in hiding. They discovered Simcha's body and were immediately suspicious that others were hiding nearby or in the building itself. How did the body just get there? Someone must have put it there. It was not there yesterday and it had been dead for a while.

That very day the Nazis sent in a team with a large dog to try smelling out the location of possible others. The dog went back and forth, back and forth, outside and inside, outside and inside. It sniffed, it went outside. It sniffed, it came back inside. It could not figure out where the smells were coming from. Back and forth, back and forth. Rachel, a few feet above where this was happening, was so frightened she could barely breathe.

The dog searched from morning until night until finally the Nazis gave up.

～

WOLF DECIDED that his family's best chance for survival was to sneak out, somehow make it to the Living Ghetto, and bring back food. His father had given him a gold watch and a gold coin from America. His plan was to use it to bribe someone to make counterfeit working papers. At the least, he would try to find food and bring it back to them.

"If I don't make it back in two days, something happened to me," he told his father ominously.

Despite the difficulty, somehow Wolf succeeded making it to the Living Ghetto and finding an apartment to stay in. No one in that apartment had working papers. They were all like him, trying to find some way to become "legal" in the Nazis' eyes.

The very next morning, the Ukrainians made a surprise inspection and caught Wolf enwrapped in his *tefillin* (the little black boxes Jewish men wear every morning during prayers). As the others staying in the apartment were all led out to be taken away, Wolf was shot outside the apartment still wearing his *tefillin*.

The Blums would find out what happened to Wolf later; meanwhile all they knew was that he hadn't returned. After two days had passed, Father told Rachel and Hannah, "Wolf isn't coming back. We can't stay here forever. We'll wait a couple of days and try to get over to the Living Ghetto."

CHAPTER 18

IN THE LIVING GHETTO

HANNAH DECIDED THAT SHE WAS NOT GOING TO SPEND ANOTHER NIGHT in the cold ceiling hideout. If she was going to die like her brothers, she was going to die trying to get out.

The next morning, she crawled down from the ceiling and walked stealthily toward the front door. After a few moments, she heard Jewish workers coming with their wagons. She peeked out of the door and got the attention of one of them. They understood her situation right away without further explanation, and motioned for her to quickly jump on the wagon and make-believe that she was one of the dead.

Hannah climbed onto the wagon and positioned herself between the corpses. She was too terrified to feel disgusted. Lying with the dead was the only way to live.

The Jewish workers pushed the wagon to the edge of the ghetto and helped Hannah off. Then, leaving the wagon behind, they walked with her — three across like the other laborers — into the Living Ghetto.

No one suspected that she was anything but another worker.

Rachel and her father — the only two left — waited an entire day. Then they decided that they too had to try to get out like Hannah.

The next morning, they crawled out of the hiding spot and found the same Jews pushing the same wagons. The workers motioned for Rachel to jump into the wagon with the other dead, and invited her father to be one of the workers pushing the wagon. Like her sister, Rachel was too frightened to think much that she was lying in a wagon with dead bodies.

At the edge of the ghetto, the workers told Rachel to get out and try to make it inside by herself. She was too young to pass as a worker, so she couldn't go in as her sister did. Luckily, she grew up in the area and knew how to navigate the backstreets. She found a small opening in the fence and snuck into the ghetto.

She wandered alone for what seemed like an eternity. until, miraculously, there was Hannah walking in the street!

"Hannah! You're alive!" Rachel said a little too loudly.

Hannah motioned her to keep her voice down and then for her to follow.

"I've been taken in by a husband and wife who have two children, a five-year-old and a newborn. They agreed to take me in because I'd be useful watching the older child, which allows the mother to attend her baby."

"Do they any room for me?" Rachel asked.

"I don't know. Let's see."

Hannah brought Rachel to the couple, but after a quick discussion they were told, "We have no room for you. And it's dangerous for us to take in another person without working papers. The Nazis regularly make raids into the ghetto's apartments asking for working papers. If someone doesn't have any, they're arrested or worse, and the family keeping them is in trouble."

"But where will I go?" Rachel asked.

The man and woman shrugged their shoulders. Rachel saw, though, that there was nothing to do. She had no choice but to return outside and search for another place.

She felt like crying, but she didn't have the luxury. She wandered the streets of the ghetto, hungry and freezing cold, her face reddened by the brutal January winds. Snow fell and whipped about the ground at her feet.

Rachel decided to enter another house. She walked up some wooden steps and found a woman in her thirties baking dough.

"Who are you?" the woman quickly asked.

"Rachel Blum. Who are you?"

"Rivka Wax."

"I'm freezing. And I'm hungry. Can I stay a little while?"

Rivka looked at the young girl and had pity on her. "Yes. Come in."

The aroma from the dough was so powerful that it permeated everything. *How did this woman get dough? And yeast?* Rachel wondered. *She must be resourceful. I must try to stay with her.*

"Please help me," Rachel finally blurted out. "I have nobody. I don't know if my father will survive and I can't stay with my sister. I'm very hungry and cold. I'm afraid if someone doesn't help me soon I'll die."

"Come take a seat," Rivka said.

"When you finish baking the bread," Rachel asked, "can I have a small piece?"

Rivka looked at the young girl in front of her. "You're not bashful, are you?"

"I am," Rachel said. "But I'm more starved than bashful."

Rivka laughed. "Yes, you can have some," she said with a friendly smile.

When the bread was done, Rivka gave Rachel a slice. Rachel savored every crumb and made it last as long as she could. It was a pleasure she would remember vividly the rest of her life.

Her joy was soon replaced by reality, though. "It's too dangerous for you to stay here very long," Rivka said. "They're always coming and checking for papers."

"Where should I go?"

"I don't know, but for your own good you have to find some other place."

Rachel stayed there about an hour, and then went back outside. She wandered around and around aimlessly.

Toward the end of the day she saw a group of Jewish men returning from work — and one of them was her father!

"Father!" she yelled as she ran over to him.

"Come with me," he said. "We'll find a place to stay."

By now it was snowing so heavily that there was no visibility. The wind whipped the snow back and forth, back and forth. Finally, Rachel and her father saw a wooden house without a door. All the windows were broken too. They walked inside. The floor was full of snow, but it was a shelter...of sorts.

"My child," Father said, "I'm exhausted. I must lie down." Without saying another word, he went over to a corner where there was very little snow, lay down, and fell asleep almost instantly.

Rachel stood there above her father for a moment — frozen physically and emotionally. What was she to do? What if he died? Where could she go?

"Oh, God," she muttered under her breath, "please help me. I'm going to freeze to death."

Then she noticed a door to another room in the wooden house. She opened it and peeked inside. It was a room full of people sleeping. However, the few beds were all occupied and every single space on the floor was taken.

She eyed a bed along one of the walls and headed toward it, hoping to find an open spot beneath it. But there was someone there too. She walked out and went to lie down near her father.

After a moment, a young man came out of the room. "My space is under the bed," he said to Rachel. "Do you want to take it?"

"Oh yes, thank you," she said. "You're an angel from Heaven."

Without hesitation, she crawled into the spot under the bed. Of course, it was still freezing cold and uncomfortable, but compared to the open foyer, the spot inside was like a five-star hotel.

In the moment before falling asleep, Rachel stopped to think how God had answered her prayer. He really listened. Then she fell into the deepest sleep.

When she woke up the next morning, everyone was gone, including her father. The people had put some chairs in front of the bed she was lying under to better hide and protect her. She stayed there until the afternoon. Then she decided to venture outside. *Maybe*

I can find Father. She doubted that he went out to work with the others because he didn't have working papers.

As Rachel walked down the empty streets of the ghetto, she noticed the open window of a cellar. It was nothing more than an empty frame. For some reason, she decided to peek inside. And there was her father!

"Father!"

"Rachel," he said excitedly, coming to the window and reaching out his arms. "Quick, come inside." She bent down and went in through the window headfirst. He caught her and deposited her gently on the floor.

"How did you find me?"

"I don't know. I just looked in."

He glanced out the window. "Did anyone see you?"

"I don't think so."

"Good. We'll make this our place for now."

Indeed, the cellar would become their "home" for the next year, from January 1943 until December 1943. The cellar had no real floor (it was earthen), doors, or windows — just openings that offered no protection from the winter elements. The howling wind blew snow back and forth the whole night, night after night. But it was a place to say.

Father tried his best to make it into a home. He gathered rocks and piled them in a corner, hoping to make a stove, but he couldn't get cement or any other materials necessary to construct a workable one. In truth, they didn't have any wood to make a fire even if he had been able to construct such a stove.

They had no blankets either. The only "luxury" was a board to sleep on. Somehow, Father found some boards and managed to bring them back to the cellar.

At first, it was only Rachel and her father in the cellar. Later, Hannah found them and joined them, at least for a while. She alternated between the family she was staying with and the cellar. The family had a small hiding place, but as long as Hannah didn't have legitimate working papers it was a risk to keep her. That's why she alternated.

Later that winter, three other people — two sisters and a brother — joined the Blums in the cellar. They had been living in the forest, moving from the land of one Polish farmer to another. The Poles had told the three siblings that Jews in the ghetto had a better chance of surviving, so the siblings snuck inside and came upon the cellar.

One of the sisters who came from the forest was named Kayla. About thirty years old, Kayla would become Rachel's protector and friend. Indeed, they would save each other's lives several times.

CHAPTER 19

IVAN'S TORMENT

IVAN ROLUK'S SECOND TIME IN TREBLINKA WAS JUST AS BAD AS THE first.

Although he didn't let others see how distraught he was, he couldn't stomach the things his eyes saw — and he had seen a lot in his life. He hated the Germans with a deep passion now.

The weather had turned decidedly cold. Winter was setting in. As Ivan pulled his trainload of Jews into the Treblinka station, he could see Jewish slave laborers dressed in thin rags. It was bad enough they had to do all the dirty work for the Germans, but they were made to suffer in every way possible at every opportunity, and the thin clothes were another way to inflict suffering.

Ivan was grateful when the train stopped and he was essentially off duty for the next few hours, after the train would be emptied of its Jews and then loaded up with clothes for the return trip to Warsaw. Ivan took out a bottle of vodka and downed the entire thing like it was water. Before he knew it, he was in a deep sleep.

When he awoke, it was already late afternoon, maybe even dusk. There was no more screaming. There were no more engine noises. He could hear activity beyond the wooden station house next to his train, but it was not the frenetic noises of earlier. It was a dull hum.

Then he heard voices coming from nearby. He wobbled out of the train and saw two Jewish slaves loading piles of clothes into the now empty train cars. A couple of Polish guards with guns, looking bored, stood over them.

When the guards saw Ivan, they asked him if he had any cigarettes. He hadn't. They asked him where he came from. He told them. Then they asked him the question they really wanted to ask: Did he have any more of that vodka? They could smell it on his breath.

Ivan showed them the empty bottle. They laughed and made a crude joke. Then they asked him if he could stand guard for a few moments. They had their own stash of vodka and wanted to get some.

"If those Jews give you trouble," they said, "just call us and we'll take care of them."

"What if any German officers come over?" Ivan asked. "They won't. They're all drunk themselves at this time in the afternoon."

"Okay, but you'll be back in a few minutes, right?"

"Right."

After the two Polish guards departed, Ivan stood there with the gun. He had no intention of shooting the Jews; he could see they weren't going to cause trouble. They just continued throwing piles of clothes into the open cattle cars.

As he stood there, Ivan wanted to see for himself what took place on the other side of the wooden station house. He'd heard about it, but he had to see it for himself. He looked at the Jews and decided they weren't going anywhere. Then he backed toward the door of the station house and opened it. As others had told him the first time, it was basically a false wall. Behind it was a more or less open area. He couldn't see everything, or even much, but what he saw confirmed everything he had heard. He saw several piles of ashes. He saw cranes lifting the ashes and depositing them into a pit. He wished he'd never awakened from his drunken stupor.

He then turned around to go back to watching the Jews working... but they weren't there! Oh, was he in trouble!

He walked over to one of the open train cars, but except for a huge pile of clothes, there was no one there. Then he went to the next open car. There too were huge piles of clothes but no Jews. As he headed for the third train he heard a noise. It came from the second open car. He looked inside and saw some of the clothes shifting, as if someone was hiding beneath them.

Ivan immediately understood the situation. The Jews hoped to escape by hiding in the train on the way back — and a part of him wanted to let them. But another part of him was afraid for himself when the guards came back and found the Jews gone.

Before he could think about it he heard someone say, "Mr. Engineer."

It was the two Polish guards, looking stunned. "Where are the Jews?"

Ivan didn't know how to react. For a second he just stood there. He glanced into the car at the pile of clothes where the Jews were hiding. Then he turned back to the guards.

"One of the Germans came by and said they were needed in the back," he told them.

The guards looked at Ivan. He looked at them. Did they believe him?

Then they laughed. "Okay."

And that was that.

CHAPTER 20

FATHER GROWS OLD BEFORE RACHEL'S EYES

WINTER SEEMED TO LAST FOREVER. RACHEL WANDERED AROUND DOING nothing, occasionally getting a scrap of food to eat or share with her father. Finally, mercifully, the winter of 1943 passed. Somehow, they had survived. As spring arrived and the weather turned nicer, Rachel and Kayla were assigned manual labor in the nearby fields. Kayla would often tell Rachel, "I see you're tired. Let me do your work. Find a quiet place where no one will see you and get some rest."

Kayla had been a farmer, and although it wasn't easy for her, she was much more accustomed to the work. Rachel was grateful that Kayla covered for her and let her go off on her own. Of course, she would make sure to come back for lunchtime — she learned to tell time by the shadow that the sun cast on the ground — when the soup was served. They called it "soup" but it really was not much more than water. However, water was good; they couldn't even get that in the ghetto.

Sometimes, Rachel would sneak away to one of the nearby farms. She would knock on the door and ask, "Do you have a little food for me?"

Even though the people suspected Rachel was Jewish, they were often willing and generous with food for her. Older Ukrainians tended to be decent. The young ones gripped in the evil of Nazi ideology were dangerous. Luckily for Rachel, most of the younger Ukrainians had been drafted into the army or police and were not present on their parents' farms.

When they gave her a piece of bread, she would take a little for herself and hide the rest under a fold in her blouse to take back to her father. Potatoes were too heavy to fit in her clothes, so she would try to eat them on the spot. But bread was something Rachel always tried to share. It kept her father alive.

After a couple of months in the fields, Rachel and Kayla were reassigned to a mason factory, which produced stone and cement used in construction. The work required was potentially backbreaking, something Rachel was not capable of performing. Luckily, there too Kayla covered for her and told her to disappear for a few hours. Rachel would return for lunchtime "soup" and scrounge some bread for herself and her father.

Father didn't have working papers and didn't want them because he felt they wouldn't save him or anyone. To the contrary, it would only make him more visible to the Germans. He realized that the Germans wanted to kill them all; it was just a matter of time. He told Rachel that he thought she was better off without the papers too.

However, by November of 1943, as the cold weather returned, the few people who remained of the Judenrat persuaded Rachel's father to register for work to get those papers. They provided him with legitimate working papers and assigned him garbage cleanup. In the very cold weather, this was extremely difficult work. All the garbage froze overnight, and Father had to take it apart with his bare hands. Without gloves, his hands froze even more. His shoes — whatever was left of them — were often wet from the snow. There was still little or no food or water, and the Blums didn't even own a pot or can to put food or water into if they could obtain a little.

Rachel's father's health deteriorated before her eyes. He didn't even look like the person she once knew. She watched this in horror but could do nothing about it.

Eventually, the ghetto organized a small infirmary in the house above the very cellar Rachel and her father had been staying in, and put him there with a few others. It was not an infirmary in the real sense of the word; there was no medicine or doctors. Mostly it was a place where people died.

CHAPTER 21

"MERRY CHRISTMAS!"

MARIA ROLUK CARRIED THE BIG POT OF PIPING HOT SOUP ACROSS THE kitchen and put it down on the table, where Ivan and Stephan were sitting expectantly. She took the ladle and first poured a generous amount into her husband's bowl. Then she took another ladleful and filled up Stephan's bowl, before finally filling up her own.

Stephan was about to be the first to dig in when his mother waved him off. "Not yet."

Ivan and Stephan then took off their fur hats.

"Let's say grace," Maria said. "Let's pray that this horrible war ends soon and that all of us find ourselves safe."

"Amen," Ivan said.

"Amen," Stephan added.

Then they all said together, "Merry Christmas!"

CHAPTER 22

RUN, RACHEL, RUN

RACHEL WAS HAVING A TERRIBLE NIGHTMARE. SHE HEARD A DISTANT voice. "Rachel." Again, "Rachel."

She opened her eyes. She was lying on the floor in a dark room, the cellar. She was grateful she had been wakened from the nightmare.

But now she was waking up to a nightmare in real life.

Shaking her awake was Kayla, her disheveled hair and rags for clothes making her look much older than she was.

"Rachel, get up!"

"Kayla?"

"Shhh. Something is happening. Listen."

Faint sounds of screaming. Then a gunshot. More screaming. Getting louder. More gunshots. Shouting. The terror-filled eyes of Rachel and Kayla met.

A single ray of light angled in from the small window high up on the far wall. Rachel got up to go toward the window. Kayla motioned for her not to, but Rachel went on and stood on her toes to look outside anyway.

At first all she saw was a ground-level view of a street. There were a few inches of snow. Then she saw people running frantically in all directions. The gunshots were louder and closer than ever.

Then, a teenage girl ran right past the window.

A moment later, a large Ukrainian man in uniform stopped in front of the window, kneeled on one knee, aimed his gun, and fired. A cruel smile flashed across his face.

Then he looked toward Rachel's direction.

However, Rachel had already crouched down. Kayla tugged at Rachel's clothes, begging her to move away from the window.

Seconds passed... seconds that seemed forever.

Rachel lifted her head as Kayla begged her not to. She looked out. The Ukrainian was gone. Rachel approached the window sill, ready to climb out. Kayla grabbed her.

"Where are you going?"

"It's not safe here."

"It's not safe out there. Are you crazy?"

"Maybe I can make it to the stream and swim across." Rachel broke free of Kayla's hold and started climbing out.

"You can't go alone."

"We can't stay here." Rachel leaned her body through the window and started crawling out.

Kayla turned back to the cellar. A teenage boy and girl were cowering in a corner: her brother and sister.

The boy said, "We're staying."

"I can't let Rachel go alone," Kayla told them.

They motioned with their hands for Kayla to go. Torn, she turned away from them and climbed out of the window to follow Rachel.

OUTSIDE, it was mayhem. People were running in all directions, shouting, hollering, screaming, and crying.

Many were running from north to south, but Rachel was running in the opposite direction, with a purpose, toward the stream. Kayla finally caught up with her and followed. They held hands and ran together.

In the distance, perhaps fifty yards ahead, they saw the stream. Its waters were white with froth, its banks blanketed in snow. The stream was too wide and deep to be waded through. It had to be swum. On the far end was an elevated bank with high grass. If they could reach the high grass they could hide or escape into the forest.

Rachel and Kayla reached the edge. For the first time, they noticed people in the stream, but the waters were too strong. An older man was struggling, drowning, being carried away in the current.

Then — gunshots.

Rachel and Kayla looked around for the source of the gunfire. In front of the brush, perhaps twenty yards upstream, across the stream, Nazis and Ukrainians had set up guns in anticipation of the Jews trying to escape.

They didn't yet notice Rachel or Kayla, but they could at any moment. They were trapped. The stream was impassable. Even if they managed to swim across it to the other side, the murderers were there waiting for them.

Suddenly, a bullet whizzed by.

Kayla reached for her neck. Rachel looked at Kayla. They shared a terrified glance. Kayla had been struck in the neck by a bullet.

Instinctively, Rachel grabbed the kerchief off Kayla's head and helped her tie it around her neck over the wound.

"We're going to die," Kayla cried.

It was a moment of truth. Rachel was terrified. She felt like giving up. What else was there to do?

And then time slowed down. Sounds were muffled. People who were running all over were moving as if in slow motion. Rachel, as if detached from herself, heard her own voice deep down inside say, *Oh, God, please don't let me die here!*

Suddenly, time and sound returned to normal. "We're not going die," Rachel told Kayla in a voice mature beyond her years, a voice even she couldn't believe was so strong.

"I'm bleeding," Kayla said.

"It's only a surface wound. You'll be okay." Rachel grabbed Kayla's hand. "Quick, we have to run. Now!"

"Where?"

"Follow me." Rachel ran with a purpose… as if a supernatural force was pushing her from behind and directing her forward.

Bullets continued to whiz by. Still holding Kayla's hand, Rachel came to a house with a wooden porch. On the porch was a bench. As if she had been there before, Rachel picked up the bench and slid back a plank. There was a hole underneath, deep enough to make the perfect hiding spot! Rachel jumped in hands- and headfirst, followed immediately by Kayla.

Rachel slid the plank cover back on top.

Thin, dust-filled rays of light through the cracks revealed the girls' tense, frightened faces. Soon they were flooded with light. Someone had pulled back the plank to expose their hiding spot.

"Who are you?" a woman asked them.

Next to her was a man, her husband. "It doesn't matter," he said to her. "Just get in."

The husband and wife, with their son of about five, quickly climbed inside the hole. A middle-aged man and woman with them also climbed in.

The wife looked at Rachel and Kayla, whose blood-stained kerchief used to cover and apply pressure to her wound made her look in much worse condition than she actually was.

"How did you get here? Who told you about this place?"

Rachel just sat quietly. Now was not the time for talking or explaining. Gunshots and shouting still rang outside. The husband put his finger on his wife's mouth, motioning to be quiet. The sound of heavy boots rattled from above on the wooden porch. Voices speaking in Ukrainian. A beam of light cast itself on Rachel's eyes. She closed them.

She heard the Ukrainians overhead ransacking the house, looking for hiding Jews. More cursing in Ukrainian. Then silence. The murderers had left.

Rachel opened her eyes. Vapor streams of cold air exited her nostrils.

The hiding place was literally a hole in the ground. There were no wooden walls nor a wooden floor. There was no room to stand up.

Rachel and the six others were huddled together. The others had their eyes closed, but were clearly breathing.

Rachel closed her eyes again. Memories flooded her mind for a second. She remembered her father — what happened to him? She remembered hearing gunshots coming from upstairs when she first crawled out of the cellar. Yes, she remembered it clearly. At the time, it didn't make sense. Now she realized what it meant.

But could she be sure? Maybe he had escaped. Should she leave the hideout and look for him? If she left they would never let her back in. It was a big risk. But it was also her father. Maybe he needed her.

Before there was time for further thinking, an overwhelming fatigue overcame her and she dozed off.

CHAPTER 23

ESCAPE IN THE SNOW

IT WAS MINUTES LATER. OR HOURS. OR DAYS. OR ETERNITIES.

Everyone in the hiding place was awake. It was still freezing cold. The husband and wife and their little boy were huddled together under several blankets. The other couple also had several blankets. Rachel and Kayla had no blankets and relied on their body heat to keep them a little warm.

The wife whispered to Kayla, "How did you find this place?"

"I didn't," Kayla replied. "She did." She motioned with her head toward Rachel.

The wife turned to Rachel. "How did you?"

"I don't know."

"What do you mean you don't know? Someone must have told you."

"I promise," Rachel said. "No one told me."

"Impossible."

"It's true," Kayla said. "She just took my hand and started running."

"An angel," Rachel interjected.

They looked at Rachel. "What?"

"An angel," Rachel told them. "I just knew I had to run here and that there was a hiding place."

The wife and husband looked at each other. After a moment, the husband removed his blanket and offered it to Rachel and Kayla.

~

MORE TIME PASSED. More eternities.

Rachel watched the little boy playing with a large glass thermometer that had its top broken off. He was using it like a shovel, digging up dirt and making a little hole.

The wife whispered to her husband, "Do you think it's safe to go outside?"

He slowly and sadly shook his head.

"Mama," the boy said loudly. "Look!"

"Shhh," his mother told him.

"Look," the boy whispered.

The boy had dug a hole deep enough to hit water, and it was filling up with a little pool. The husband grabbed the thermometer, shook out some of the dirt, and dipped it in. Then he slowly took a sip.

The others waited longingly to see his reaction. He rolled the water around in his mouth, then nodded his head and motioned that it was good. The mother clasped her hands in thankfulness.

Within a day, the little hole had become the size of a kitchen sink, filled with f water. The wife handed Rachel the thermometer filled with the dirty but life-giving liquid.

By the next day, the little hole had grown into a deep tub, but the water was coming in much too fast. Rachel whispered to Kayla, "We can't stay here. At night, we go out."

~

THE NIGHT SKY WAS MOONLESS, and even though there was snow on the ground, Rachel and Kayla took off their boots to muffle their steps as they walked.

They darted behind house after house until they came to the edge of the ghetto, heading for the cemetery. Then they put on their boots

— their socks and feet were soaking wet and freezing. But they had not been noticed. They held hands and walked out of the ghetto and into the cemetery.

A Ukrainian policeman yelled at them, "Stop! Where are you going?"

"Home," Rachel replied.

He gave them a look and let them go.

They walked through the cemetery. "There's a single mother I know," Rachel told Kayla. "My father used to pay her to help do our laundry. I know where her house is. She has a daughter my age. Maybe she'll have pity on us."

They arrived at the house and knocked on the door. The woman immediately recognized Rachel and invited her in, even starting a fire to warm them up.

"It's very generous of you to keep us," Rachel said.

"It's very dangerous for me to keep you," the woman told Rachel and Kayla. "And I have barely enough food for myself and my daughter."

Silence.

"You can stay with me for a while," the woman said to Rachel, "but I can't keep both of you." She glanced at Kayla.

Kayla looked at Rachel, then at the woman. "Where can I go?" she asked.

"There are Jewish partisans in the forest. I can tell you how to find them."

Even the best partisans — Poles, Russians, and Jews who had escaped to the forest — were very violent people. They had to be. They didn't tolerate people who couldn't help, to say nothing of a person who got sick; that would be the end of them.

Nevertheless, Kayla found her way to the partisans. When they asked her what she could do to help them, she told them she could cook, clean clothes, and keep guard duty. They kept her and she survived the war with them.

CHAPTER 24

RUMORS

MARIA ROLUK LISTENED WITH HORROR AS HER NEIGHBOR TOLD THE story.

"One of the Nazis, I think his name was Wassterheide, organized a kidnapping operation to send Poles to Germany for forced labor. And who was helping him? Jews. Can you believe it? Jews helping Nazis kidnap Poles."

"Can't be," another neighbor said.

"Are there any Jews left?" asked another.

"Oh yes," the first neighbor replied. "They're hiding. But they're around."

"Yeah, but if the Nazis found them they'd kill them. It doesn't make sense that they're helping Nazis."

"Well, I don't know. Maybe they're letting some of them live."

"But if they did, why would the Nazis let Jews do anything?"

"I don't know, but they did."

"I don't believe it. It makes no sense."

"It sounds to me like an unfounded rumor," Maria piped in. "A wild, unfounded rumor. But even if it's true, those Jews would have no choice."

"Why do you say it's a rumor, Maria?" the first neighbor asked. "Why would they spread such a thing?"

"To make us hate. To make us seek revenge even more."

"Revenge for what?"

"So we'll inform on any last Jews hiding."

The women were quiet.

"How do you know this?" one of the women asked.

"I don't," Maria replied.

"It makes sense," another woman added. "Maria's right. The Nazis want us to hate and hate and hate."

"But are there really any more Jews to hate?" one of the neighbors said, repeating her earlier question.

"Not many. But they're out there, hiding."

"It's true," the first woman said. "Just yesterday I heard this story. There was a Jewish man and woman hiding on a farm. When the farmer's friend found out about them, the farmer killed the Jews."

"How do you know this?"

"The farmer confessed to the priest because he felt guilty. Now he tells everyone about it and how he's absolved." Everyone was quiet.

After the war, Rachel would find out that her sister, Hannah, who had escaped the ghetto before the final liquidation, found temporary shelter at a farm. After she stayed there a while, the farmer murdered her and another Jew, confessed his crime to a priest, and boasted to everyone what he had done.

CHAPTER 25

KARINA

THE SINGLE WOMAN WHO ALLOWED RACHEL TO STAY IN HER HOUSE HAD a daughter, Karina, about Rachel's age. Rachel and Karina had known each other before the war. After Rachel's mother died, her father had been forced to hire help for around the house. Karina's mother often came to the Blum house to do their laundry. Since she usually brought Karina with her, she and Rachel got to know each other. The two shared much in common despite their religious differences.

~

ONE DAY, Rachel convinced Karina to go for a walk with her. They had already agreed on the alibi: if anyone asked who Rachel was, she was Karina's cousin from a faraway town who was staying over for a while as her parents dealt with the difficulties of the war. It was good for Rachel to get out, and perhaps they would be able to find some extra food too.

It was late in the afternoon when they crossed near the now liquidated Jewish ghetto. Suddenly, two policemen appeared and approached them. One was German and the other was Ukrainian.

"Where are you going?" the Ukrainian asked.

"We're just going through."

"Why aren't you in school?"

"We have no school."

"What are you doing here?"

"We're just walking. Then we're going home."

The German said to the Ukrainian, in German, "Are they Jews?" Even at this stage, the Germans were looking to get every last Jew.

The Ukrainian then looked at the girls and said, "He just asked me if you're Jews."

Rachel was terrified but tried not to show it. "Listen," she told the Ukrainian firmly. "I'm just like your sister. If you shoot us, it's as if you're shooting your sisters." Then she started to cry.

"Let them go," the German said to the Ukrainian.

They let them go, but Rachel was suspicious of the Ukrainian. She suspected that he would follow them. She convinced Karina that they should go home through the Jewish ghetto — the Death Ghetto — that Rachel knew so well, and dart into a building that she remembered had a hiding place.

That's what they did. When they got there, Rachel showed Karina the hiding place. She pulled back a blanket behind a cabinet.

"Let's crawl into this hiding place," Rachel said.

They went inside. Not a moment later there was a noise. Through the cracks, they saw that the Ukrainian had followed them. He was inside, not far from their hiding spot. Holding his rifle, he moved around some debris lying about. The room had two doors, one in the front and one in the back. He exited through the back, assuming the girls had gone out that way.

They waited and waited and waited. When they were sure the coast was clear, they left and made a beeline for home.

From then on, Rachel decided she was never going to go out unless she absolutely had to.

CHAPTER 26

DISCOVERED!

RACHEL HAD BEEN HIDING WITH KARINA AND HER MOTHER FOR ABOUT A month. One day, while Rachel was home alone and washing clothes, suddenly a man appeared at the window and looked in. It was that Ukrainian guard who had stopped her and Karina!

Rachel scampered into the bedroom and hid under the bed, but she had been seen. She stayed under the bed for hours. When Karina's mother came home she saw Rachel hiding. "What are you doing there?"

Rachel then told her about the man who had peeked in the window.

"That one's a real Jew hater," she told Rachel. "It's no longer safe to stay here. Listen, you can stay tonight, but in the morning, you'll have to go."

"Go?" Rachel said, gulping. "Where?"

"Any place. After a week or two, come back and I'll take you in again."

Rachel was terrified. Where could she go? How would she survive?

CHAPTER 27

THE DREAM

That night Rachel could hardly sleep. In a few hours, she would have to leave and be completely on her own. No mother. No father. No siblings. No Kayla. No Karina's mother. No Karina. She would be a little girl alone in a world bent on destroying her.

She tossed and turned in bed... until finally, mercifully, she fell asleep.

Sleeping very deeply... she dreamed.

She dreamed of a dark, dark night in the freezing cold Ukrainian winter. A full moon in the sky reflected an eerie light. There was a hill. At the top was an old-fashioned water pump with a wooden trough.

A little girl walked up the hill carrying a metal pail in each hand. It was Rachel. Her clothes were tattered and not nearly warm enough. She looked behind her to the left. Her nose and cheeks were flushed red.

A noise.

She stopped. She looked behind her. A deathly quiet. She turned forward and continued up the hill. She reached the top and put down one of the pails. She leaned over the trough and looked inside the well. In the moonlight, it was plainly visible that the water was frozen. She took one of the pails and placed it under the pump. Then she began pumping. Nothing happened; no water came up. She pumped more vigorously, pumping and pumping. Nothing happened...

Finally, a little water oozed out.

But it wasn't normal water. It was black, an ugly black. It was unnatural. Rachel recoiled. Before she could do anything, the black water froze. The spout of the pump was caked with the ugly, frozen water. She was horrified. Distraught.

How could she go back with dirty water? They're going to kill her. Rachel started to cry. "What am I going to do now?"

At that moment, her father, looking luminous, appeared in the dream.

"Listen, my child," he said. "Pour out this dirty water and give me the pails."

He spilled out the dirty water and filled two pails of clean water. Then he said, "Go, my child, and don't be afraid. Everything will be all right. Go home."

Rachel was awakened by Karina's mother.

"Almost morning," she said. "Time to go."

CHAPTER 28

KNITTING FOR DISTRACTION

Maria Roluk had been knitting for hours. Usually it was a surefire way to calm her nerves, but ever since Ivan had assaulted — almost killed — Stephan, her nerves were more fragile than usual, although you wouldn't necessarily know it on the outside. She always managed to keep her calm, aristocratic exterior.

There was much to worry about. Ivan told her how the war was going badly for the Germans. What did that mean for Stephan? If the Russians, indeed, swept the Germans away and rolled in, how would they view his work in the SS office? Would they understand that he did it because he had no choice? And that the work he did was clerical and nothing more? She knew the Russians, and she suspected they might not.

Since the knitting was not calming her nerves, she put it down. Enough knitting. Enough sitting. "I have to get out and get some air," she muttered under her breath. "Let me go out to the barn and feed the horses or something."

She looked around her house. No one was home. "Now you're talking to yourself, out loud," she said and laughed at herself.

With that, she picked herself up and walked out the front door.

CHAPTER 29

THE BARN

ALTHOUGH RACHEL WAS MORE ALONE THAN EVER AND HAD LOST everybody, the dream of her father had changed everything. Suddenly, she had a renewed feeling of confidence. She didn't know if she would live or die, but whatever would be, would be. Everything was going to be okay. That's what her father had said in the dream, and she believed it. There was no reason to worry. Whatever happened yesterday was finished. Rachel's only thought was how to make it better for today and tomorrow. That was her new philosophy in life.

She walked down a crowded cobblestone street, surrounded by people on their way to work. She had a feeling as she walked that everyone's eyes were watching her. She'd done her best to clean up, but maybe she'd missed something. Maybe her clothes or her hair made her look even more unkempt than an average girl during wartime. She shivered. The worst thing that could happen to her was to be noticed. She had to get out of sight.

Looking around, she saw a yard with a barn in the back. Even better, there didn't seem to be a dog in the yard, so she wouldn't have to worry about barking giving her away. It seemed like a good hiding place.

Rachel made her way to the barn door and opened it slowly. Peering inside, she saw a cow in one corner, a goat in another, and a bale of dried hay in another. Better and better. She settled herself next to the bale, burying her feet in the hay to warm them up. She whispered a silent prayer that no one would come into the barn. She just needed a little time to rest and warm up; then she would figure out what to do next.

At that very moment, the barn door opened and a woman stepped inside. She looked at Rachel, and Rachel looked right back at her. Before the woman could say anything, Rachel blurted, "Don't worry, I won't stay forever. Please don't tell anyone I'm here. I'll be gone by the morning."

The woman gave Rachel a long look and then went about her business, first milking the goat and then the cow, as if no one else was there. Then, without saying a word, she left and closed the barn. Rachel let out a sigh of relief.

CHAPTER 30

NOTHING TO LOSE

THE DAY PASSED UNEVENTFULLY FOR RACHEL. AS DARKNESS SETTLED, however, a feeling of dread enveloped her. Maybe she had a place to spend the night in relative safety, but she'd promised to be gone by the morning, and she had no idea where to go. It was so cold. And she was so alone. She wanted to cry, but she knew that wouldn't help. Rachel held on to the image of her father telling her that everything would work out. She just had to keep going.

She thought about the woman who had come into the barn. She hadn't seemed to mind that Rachel was there, but there was no way to be sure, and a mistake in trusting the woman could be the difference between life and death.

Rachel decided she had nothing to lose. Continuing into the unknown, in the freezing winter, she picked herself up off the floor, brushed off the hay, and headed out the barn door. The freezing air hit her face, and the wind blew some of the surface snow at her. She saw a shallow path in the snow, where the woman must have walked from her house to the barn, and Rachel slowly made her way along that path, putting her feet into the woman's shoeprints. The house wasn't far, but the snow was deep and her shoes didn't offer much protection.

By the time Rachel reached the house, she was shaking so much from the cold that she could barely form a fist to knock. It didn't matter. She couldn't stand outside waiting for anyone to answer the door. Someone might see her, and besides, she was already half-frozen. She took a deep breath, praying for courage, and opened the door to the house.

She saw the family sitting around a table: the woman, a man, and a teenage boy. Rachel's courage failed her, and she couldn't take the step inside. She just stood there in the doorway, frozen by fear and the bone-deep chill. She knew she needed to say something, do something, but couldn't.

The woman turned to see who had opened the door, and she looked startled. Startled, but not angry. Rachel let out a breath she didn't even know she had been holding. The woman motioned to her. "Come inside, child. Close the door. It's cold outside."

Turning to her husband, the woman said, "This is the girl I found in the barn this morning. She must be cold. And hungry."

The man nodded. He got up and pulled a chair over to the table. "Sit down, child. Tell us your name."

Rachel watched as the woman got up to put some food on a plate. Rachel's mouth watered. Hot food. It had been a long time since her last hot meal.

They were all watching her. Rachel blinked. The man had asked something. Right. Her name.

"My name is Rachel," she said. "Rachel Blum."

"Blum?" the woman said with genuine surprise. "Did your father make vinegar?"

"Yes. How did you know?"

"We used to do business with him. He'd give us a few bottles of vinegar to sell without paying any money upfront. Whenever we sold some, we paid him. He was satisfied with that arrangement. Sometimes he'd come over, and we'd sit and talk for hours. He was a very fine man."

They knew her father! Her father, who only the previous night had come to Rachel's dream to tell her not to be afraid. A chill traveled down Rachel's spine and she felt a "Hidden Hand" in her life, right there in the middle of all the death and destruction.

With this sense of faith, she blurted out something to her hosts that even she was surprised came out of her lips. "Do you have a Bible?"

The woman looked at the man, and the man at the woman. "Of course."

"Please, can you bring it to the table here?"

The man took it off the shelf and brought it over.

"Please, everyone, sit," Rachel said. "Everyone, put your hands on this Bible."

They did as she asked, not sure what would come out of this little girl's mouth next.

"I have nowhere to go after tonight," Rachel said. "I can't run any longer. If you tell me I can stay, I'll stay. If you tell me to leave, I'll leave. But if you tell me to leave, I'll tell you that I have no more strength to run. Instead, I'll go behind your barn, lie down in the snow, fall asleep, and die. And maybe the snow will bury me, or maybe you'll be kind enough to dig me a proper grave. But for me, this is the end."

Rachel scanned their faced for a reaction. It was hard to tell. They were quiet, so she continued.

"We all know that one day this war will end. And there will be some Jews who survive, with God's help. Now, I want you to swear on this Bible that after the war you'll find Jews and tell them. Tell them that there was a Jewish girl buried here. Tell them to dig up my body and rebury it in a Jewish cemetery, so I can be with my people. Promise me. Swear to me on this Bible."

The family sat there, stunned by Rachel's words. They looked at each other, speechless. Rachel sat, terrified, waiting for a reaction, any reaction. They all sat in silence for a minute.

Two minutes.

Two minutes that seemed an eternity.

Finally, the woman said to her husband, "We have to keep her. If she made it all the way until now, we have to make sure she lives."

The man nodded. "It may be a small thing, but it is something. It's something we can do. I've seen too much in this war. I can't be responsible for this child's death."

They looked at their son, and he nodded too. "I might not have a sister, but it would be nice to have a cousin."

"We're agreed, then," the woman added. Turning to Rachel, she said, "We'll keep you as long as we can."

"What is your name?" Rachel asked.

"My name is Maria," the woman answered.

"And my name is Ivan," the man said.

"And my name is Stephan," the teenage boy added.

"We are the Roluks," Maria told Rachel.

CHAPTER 31

THE SS ARRIVE

IN APRIL 1944, A NEW CONTINGENT OF GERMAN SOLDIERS SUDDENLY showed up one night in Ludmir. Their uniforms were black and their caps were adorned with a skull- and-crossbones insignia. History knows this symbol as the *Totenkopf* which is German for "death's head" or "skull and bones." It was the symbol of the infamous SS *(Schutzstaffel)*.

They represented the evilest aspects of Nazism. The SS were not only responsible for the most of the worst war crimes, but ran the concentration camps and enacted the Holocaust.

As soon as they arrived in Ludmir, they immediately began burning down farms. The partisans often relied on farmers, willingly or unwillingly, to supply them with food. The SS didn't care if the farmers hadn't helped any partisans; they were there to destroy their farms whether they did or did not.

The first week the SS arrived, they burned the farms owned by Poles. During the next week, they set fire to the farms of the Ukrainians, even though the Ukrainians were less inclined to help partisans, certainly not Jewish ones but even Polish ones. Perhaps some had, or perhaps the Nazis just wanted to put fear in everyone. They didn't need excuses to do so.

⸎

THE DAY after the SS troops first arrived, they told the Roluks and others to leave their homes, because their homes were near the farms and the Germans were now going to occupy them as part of their fight against the partisans.

Luckily, Maria Roluk knew of an empty house to move into. It was once the home of a wealthy Jew. It had five rooms and two kitchens. There was also a large garden in the back with a creek running through it and a well.

Early one morning in their new place of residence, Rachel heard a commotion and looked out the window. There she saw a group of about five hundred skinny, disheveled prisoners dressed with sacks on their feet instead of shoes, and in rags on their backs serving as clothing, being led down the street. They were Jews on what history would later call a "death march."

"They are Hungarian Jews," people in the market told Maria. No one knew where they were being marched to or what happened to them, but the image of their pitiful plight remained etched in everyone's memory.

CHAPTER 32

THE ENCROACHING FRONT

ONE DAY IN EARLY SUMMER, STEPHAN ROLUK CAME HOME FROM WORK in the SS office and told the family that he heard the Nazis were suffering huge defeats.

Indeed, at 5:00 a.m. on June 22, 1944 — exactly three years to the day that the Germans launched their surprise attack against the Russians — the Red Army launched a gargantuan surprise attack against the Germans.

Ivan Roluk had earlier learned how bad the war was going for the Germans from his work driving trains for them to the front. After the wounded were loaded onto his train, he drove them back to safer areas. As time passed, it became obvious to him that the front was getting closer and closer. Each time he had to drive less of a distance to the front than the previous time.

Of course, he was forbidden to tell anyone how badly things were going for the Nazis. Even though there were not too many men with knowledge of the intricacies of train travel to replace Ivan, the Nazis would kill him and his family if it was leaked and traced back to him. In fact, the Germans made sure to accompany him home from the train station each night and monitor who he spoke to. They didn't let him go anywhere alone.

Although they couldn't tell anyone else, the Roluks knew how close the front was coming. The thought gave them hope.

CHAPTER 33

STARED DOWN BY A NAZI GENERAL

ONE MORNING, RACHEL WENT INTO THE BACKYARD TO GET WATER FROM the well near the creek. It was an idyllic setting. The water was crystal clear. The rhythmic sound of the creek's waters so peaceful.

It was so peaceful, in fact, that for a moment she forgot that on the other side of the creek was a large, well-built stone house where the SS was stationed. It was an unusual house because it had large electric poles with wires leading into it. The Russians had wired the house for communications between 1939 and 1941. The Germans had taken over the house and made it the headquarters for their own communications network in the area. Rachel felt uncomfortable living next door to Nazis, but there was nothing she could do about it.

As she was bending over the pail of water she had filled, she heard a strange voice say, "Water."

She looked up. It was a tall, dark, intimidating man in a black SS uniform. She saw the skull- and-crossbones symbol on his black hat. She saw three stars on his lapel. She could even see a big green leaf on his uniform. (Later, Ivan Roluk would explain to her that the three stars meant he was a general, and the green leaf signified that he had fought in the epic Battle of Stalingrad.)

Even without knowing his precise rank, Rachel froze. She couldn't lift her head. The SS general came closer and repeated, "Give me the pail of water." Rachel was still too terrified to move.

The Nazi blurted, "You look very suspicious to me, little girl." Then he added, "Are you a Jew?"

Rachel instantly dropped the pail, ran into the house, and zoomed past Ivan. Without waiting for him, she ran out the back door as fast as she could and leaped across the creek into a swampy area with tall grass just in front of the woods.

Indeed, the SS general came back later that morning with a German shepherd. He told the Roluks that he suspected that Rachel was a Jew.

"What do you think," Ivan said with a laugh, "that there are any Jews left in Ludmir? You got them all, Herr General. No, she is the daughter of my wife's sister. Her parents were killed and her farm destroyed, so she moved in with us."

The German believed him, or so it seemed, and left.

Later that day, when the sun started going down, Ivan came to the edge of the woods and called out to Rachel, "It's safe. You can come out now."

Rachel emerged from the swampy brush. Looking at the creek she realized it was too wide too cross. Instead, Ivan placed a piece of lumber and laid it across for her to walk over. (Rachel would later tell people that she didn't know how she leaped across the creek in the first place. "It was a miracle," she would say.)

That whole night Rachel couldn't sleep. Neither could the Roluks. Perhaps the SS general didn't believe Ivan and would come back while they were sleeping.

It is worthwhile to pause a moment and examine the incredible, irrational hatred known as anti-Semitism. The Nazis were on the verge of defeat. The Russians were perhaps a few days away. Yet, this general — a decorated German warrior with medals for bravery — was worried that perhaps this little girl was Jewish. Despite everything else he had to deal with, his mind was still consumed with the thought of finding and killing every last Jew!

CHAPTER 34

MOVING OUT

THE SS GENERAL DIDN'T HAVE TIME INVESTIGATE FURTHER BECAUSE THE very next day he got orders to move his troops out of Ludmir. He ordered Ivan to put together a train for about five hundred wounded soldiers — the equivalent of about ten train cars — to be brought west.

"I can't go with you if my family can't come with me," Ivan said. The Nazi agreed and let him add one car at the end of the train for his wife, son, and Rachel.

(History records the day the Russians liberated Ludmir on July 22, 1944, just two days after German officers tried to assassinate Hitler. However, Rachel and the Roluks left on the train with the Germans about a week or two before the Russians arrived.)

They headed west and soon arrived in Hrubieszow (pronounced "Ruby-eshev"), a town on the border of the original Russian-German armistice line of 1939. Ivan was ordered to pull the train into the station and prepare to pick up more wounded soldiers, at least twice as many. To do so, he now needed to find at least ten more train cars. Then he would be able to take the very large transport of perhaps one thousand wounded soldiers further west toward the city of Lublin.

It was not simple finding those extra cars. It would take him a couple of days, he told the SS general. The wounded who couldn't move stayed on the train, but those who could and about twenty non-wounded soldiers disembarked. Maria, Stephan, and Rachel also got off the train but stayed in a park a short distance away.

The next morning, Rachel woke up to the smell of hot bread and coffee. A German soldier was standing at the head of a line apportioning the rations to other soldiers. As naive as she was desperate — but most of all, hungry — Rachel got on line and waited her turn. When it came, the German gave her a look. She looked back at him.

"She doesn't look like a Pole," he said to a soldier next to him. "She looks like a Jew."

Oh, God, Rachel thought, *please don't let him recognize me. Let me walk away as if nothing happened.* Her prayer was answered. The cook gave her a small amount of bread and a coffee, and motioned for her to go.

By now, however, Rachel was afraid not only of the SS general but of every German. Somehow, they suspected she was Jewish. When she returned to Maria, she told her what had happened and said, "I'm never going for food anymore. I'm too afraid."

CHAPTER 35

OFF TO WARSAW

IVAN TRIED HIS BEST TO FIND THE EXTRA TEN CARS, BUT THERE WERE few to be had. Most trains that passed through were heading east, toward the front. Finally, after almost a week, and with a threat from the SS general, they commandeered train cars from a transport that pulled into the station. The wounded and everyone else, including Maria, Stephan, and Rachel, were loaded into the now twenty-car-long train and they departed.

The final destination was to be the city of Warsaw, still occupied by the Germans. In addition to a command center, it also had one of the best hospitals. On the way there, they had to pass through Lublin, a major city occupied by the Germans, although not as large as Warsaw.

The trip from Hrubieszow to Lublin normally took only a few hours. However, almost as soon as the train left Hrubieszow the skies were filled with Russian planes. Although their train was supposedly safe, because it was clearly marked as a Red Cross train and visible from the sky, even if the Russians had abided by the rules of war, a bomb could have easily strayed off course, or in the fog the pilot might mistake the train for a military convoy. Either way, Ivan had to proceed very cautiously. When he heard planes, he stopped the train and kept it under the cover of woods.

A trip of a few hours turned into a day. and then two days... and then three.

CHAPTER 36

RACHEL'S DARING PLAN

FINALLY, ON THE THIRD DAY, IVAN SAW THE OUTSKIRTS OF LUBLIN IN the distance. However, the train could not enter because a battle was already raging on the city's outskirts. The Germans repelled the Russians and forced them to temporarily bypass Lublin. Nevertheless, since Ivan had already driven the train into the area it was now not possible to continue into Lublin itself. Therefore, he stopped it some distance outside the city.

"Change in plans," the SS general told Ivan. "We can't go to Warsaw. The Russians have bombed the railway lines. Our new instructions are to proceed to Stettin, in Germany proper, and from there to Berlin."

"With your permission," Ivan replied, "I would like to tell my family in the caboose."

"Permission granted. We have to finish burying the dead anyway." About ten of the wounded soldiers had died along the way and now needed burial. "But don't take long. When we blow the horn, I want you back here in an instant."

"Yes, Herr General."

Ivan walked at a brisk pace to the caboose. Emotion was not easy for him, but he felt a sense of elation seeing his family each time, knowing that death could come upon them at any minute.

"Why have we stopped?" Maria asked.

"All the tracks in and out of the city are being bombed. We were supposed to go to Warsaw but it's impossible now. The Germans have given me new instructions. We're going to Stettin, and from there to Berlin."

Berlin… the capital of Nazi Germany! Rachel's heart sunk as she heard the words.

"No," she blurted out with a conviction that surprised even her.

The Roluks looked at her.

"You know what the Germans are," she continued. "How can you even think of going with them? I'm not going. I'm staying here."

Maria looked at her husband, imploring him to say something. Finally, he said to Rachel, "I know the Germans are no good. But what choice do we have?"

"We have a choice."

"What?"

"There is always a choice."

"What?" They looked at her skeptically.

Rachel looked Ivan squarely in the eyes and finally said, "No one knows these tracks better than you. You know every turn and bend. You'll drive the train as you normally do. When there's a sharp curve up ahead you'll slow down. You'll blow your horn three times. We'll jump off. Then you'll speed up into the curve so that the train will topple over, and you'll jump off at the last moment."

There was silence. Stony silence. Ivan broke it first. "It's a crazy idea."

"Why?"

"It's too risky."

"There are risks either way. If we stay with the Germans all the way to Berlin — if the train doesn't get bombed along the way — who knows what they'll do to you."

Ivan took a deep breath. He looked at his wife. He looked at his son. He looked at Rachel. "No," he said definitively.

"You've been driving trains for the Nazis for three years now," Rachel said. "You know exactly who they are. You know there are no more Jews in Ludmir. And don't think they'll stop with Jews. Once we're in Berlin, they'll kill you too?"

"No, they'll need me to drive their trains."

"And if they don't need your services?"

"No, your idea is too risky."

"It is a risk to do it, but also a risk not to."

Ivan looked at his wife. Then at Stephan. Suddenly, there was a loud blast from the horn. The Germans were letting him know it was time to get going.

"Okay," he told him family. "When I see the next big curve in the tracks, I'll blow the horn three times. That'll be your signal to jump. But you'll only have a few seconds to jump before I pick up speed."

Ivan and Maria looked at each other.

Another loud blast from the horn.

"The Germans are impatient. I must go."

As Maria, Stephan, and Rachel watched Ivan return to the front of the train, they climbed onto the caboose.

A couple of minutes later, the train jerked forward and pulled out of the waiting area.

CHAPTER 37

NO TIME FOR FEAR

Ten minutes later. Or is it ten hours? Ten lifetimes?

Rachel, Maria, and Stephan sit quietly and tense in the caboose. The only sound is the click-click, click-click of the train moving along the tracks.

After what seems like an eternity, the train seems to slow down.

Maria opens the door to the caboose. A rush of air whooshes inside. They step out to the ledge. There's a ditch to the side of the train tracks and beyond it a line of trees passing by in a blur of green.

The train slows even more.

Then there's a blow of the horn. and another. and finally a third.

It's the signal. The time has come.

Each of them has a sack filled with a little bit of food. They look at each other and jump.

Rachel hits the ground and rolls into a ditch, followed by Maria and Stephan. Rachel is the first to look up. Everyone is okay.

Then they watch the train speed up.

The train continues to pick up speed as it heads down the tracks.

They watch... and watch... and watch.

Meanwhile, in the front, Ivan is having doubts. The train is too long for him to see if his family jumped out. Maybe they got scared and didn't jump. Maybe this was a really bad idea.

On one level, he knows that the time to debate the issue has passed. He knows this part of the tracks leading into Lublin like the back of his hand, and less than a few seconds away is a sharp bend.

He looks behind him. The twenty train cars filled with over one thousand wounded Nazis snakes behind his engine car like a meandering river. Slowing down is normal procedure for a train coming upon a sharp bend, of course.

He looks back again. Did they jump out of the caboose?

He hears a door open. What is that? It sounds like the door connecting the engine car to the first passenger car, with the SS general and other high-ranking Nazis. Is one of them coming to the front?

The moment of truth has arrived.

Ivan takes a deep breath of air and thrusts the throttle full ahead.

The train jerks ahead.

He looks out the window. There's the bend! Did he wait too long? If so, the train won't tip over. And even if he timed it right, will he be able to roll clear of the capsizing train wreck?

There is no more time to think. There is no more time for fear. He leans out the open side door... and jumps!

CHAPTER 38

THE TIPPING POINT

IVAN ROLLS DOWN THE SLANTED GRAVEL SIDE OF THE TRACKS AND INTO a grass ditch. Then he watches the train.

It rolls along... and rolls... and rolls.

Suddenly, the great monster tips... and there's a thunderous crash! One by one, all twenty cars of the train flop over on their sides. Then there's an explosion. The trains are all on fire!

Far away, Maria, Rachel, and Stephan hear the explosion. It's hard to imagine how anyone could survive. They look pensively toward the billowing smoke. Especially Maria. Is her husband okay? Did he make it?

Minutes pass. Still no sign of Ivan.

More minutes pass. Then, up ahead, along the ditch, they see a shadow in the distance.

Ivan!

He reaches Maria and Stephan. He takes a look at Rachel. The Jewish girl's crazy plan worked.

As he crouches with them in the ditch, he looks at his handiwork — the broken train — and lets out a huge sigh of relief. Tears stream down Rachel's cheeks. They are free of the Germans.

At least for now.

CHAPTER 39

"POLES"

THE DANGER IS FAR FROM OVER. WAR BETWEEN THE GERMANS AND Russians is now raging inside Lublin and the surrounding country-side. Moreover, Ivan and Maria don't know Polish. The Poles hate Russians. Who knows what they would do if they found out their true identities?

Ivan and Maria also fear approaching the Russians because front-line soldiers are known to be the most brutal, trigger-happy, and reckless. They kill on a whim. Young or old, man or woman, civilian or other — it doesn't matter: they kill.

Rachel and Stephan, however, speak perfect Polish. They decide to venture toward the outskirts of Lublin while Ivan and Maria stay in the ditch.

After a short while, Rachel and Stephan find a woman and speak to her in Polish. The woman has no idea that she is speaking to a Jew and a Russian. "We just escaped from the Germans and have no place to stay. Can you help us?"

"Yes," she said, happy to help some fellow "Poles." "I have no room in my house, but next to it I have a slaughterhouse. All my animals were long ago taken by the Germans. If you want to stay there you can. The floor is concrete, but you can lock yourself inside and stay there until things calm down."

"Can we get our parents?"

"Yes."

Rachel and Stephan return to the ditch to tell Maria and Ivan that they found a house to stay in… temporarily.

CHAPTER 40

THE BATTLE OF LUBLIN

IVAN, MARIA, STEPHAN, AND RACHEL STAY LITERALLY LOCKED INSIDE the slaughterhouse for a week. During that time, the Germans and Russians are locked in one of the fiercest battles of the war, one later called the Battle of Lublin.

Artillery and armor fire incessantly. Tanks clash in the open. Planes bomb defenses continually day and night. The city is devastated. An inferno of flame and gunfire engulf the Nazi defenders. The final, desperate job is performed by the Russian infantry. Russian soldiers storm Lublin, street by street, shooting anyone not in a Russian uniform. The fighting is house to house, hand to hand. It's a fight to the finish.

Finally, one day the bombing and gunfire stop. The battle is over.

But the Roluks aren't sure who won. Tentatively, Rachel ventures outside with Stephan. Not far from the backyard of the slaughter-house is a wooded area. They hear some commotion and quietly make their way through thick bushes. In a clearing beyond the thicket they see a thousand — perhaps thousands of — German prisoners of war under guard, looking exhausted, dirty, depressed. Beaten.

The Russians won! They control Lublin!

The next morning, Rachel and Stephan sneak through the woods to the same wooded area. The German prisoners are still there — but now they're surrounded by a barbwire fence. The Russians have confiscated their boots, uniforms, and whatever valuables they had hidden on their bodies.

Soon the Russians will do to the Germans what the Germans did to others.

CHAPTER 41

"THEY BURN JEWS"

ONE NIGHT RACHEL IS SITTING WITH THE POLISH WOMAN WHO OWNS the slaughterhouse and some of her friends. They speak about war, loved ones, and the future. At one point in the conversation, Rachel hears one of the women say, "Do you smell that horrible smell?"

"Yes," her friend says.

"It's the Jews," another woman interjects.

Rachel isn't sure she heard correctly.

"The Jews?" one of the other women asks.

"Yes."

None of the Polish women know or even suspect that the girl sitting right there with them, Rachel, is herself Jewish.

The woman continues, "There's a camp a few miles from here on the outskirts of the city called Majdanek [pronounced "My-da-neck"]. It's surrounded by barbed wire. In there they send Jews, gas them to death, and then burn them in ovens."

Rachel sits there in shock, but doesn't dare say anything. It's the first she's heard of such things. It's impossible to believe. How could it be?

The next day, Rachel mentions the conversation to Ivan. "I heard last night that there's a place not far from here where they've been killing Jews. I have to go see it. Please come with me."

"No, I'm not going there."

"I beg you."

"Please don't ask me."

"But I have to go. I have to see it with my own eyes. If you don't take me, I'll go myself."

Ivan realizes that Rachel is serious and agrees to go with her.

CHAPTER 42

MAJDANEK

EVEN BEFORE THE FIGHTING BETWEEN THE GERMANS AND RUSSIANS RAGING in Lublin finished, the Russians made a shocking discovery in a suburb just to the east, not far from Lublin — Majdanek. Although originally constructed as a slave labor camp, it eventually became a death camp with gas chambers and crematoria (buildings for incinerating the dead). Rachel Blum would be one of the first civilians, and probably the first Jewish civilian, to see it with her own eyes....

Rachel and Ivan leave Lublin early in the morning, each with a loaf of bread. Columns of trucks packed with Russian soldiers are streaming in the opposite direction, toward Warsaw, in preparation for the battle that was to take place there. There isn't even a single truck heading in their direction; there is no one to ask for a ride.

It takes an hour or so on foot to reach Majdanek — not only because of the distance and the extreme heat but because it was a literal war zone the day or two before. Along the way there are dead bodies from all sides: Germans, Russians, civilians — even horses. The roads are littered thick with the dead, as there was no time to bury any of them.

At one point Rachel and Ivan see a stopped Russian tank with a soldier sitting lazily on top of it. "Do you know where the Majdanek camp is?" Rachel asks.

He looks at them pathetically and points back in the direction where he came from.

They walk and walk until they finally arrive at the front gate of the concentration camp late in the afternoon.

The entrance is graced by beautiful green grass and magnificent gardens. There is also a lovely house just beyond the gate, which probably housed the German officers. It was truly a picturesque scene... except for the infamous inscription across the gate, *Work makes free.*

History marks the day of liberation of Majdanek as July 23, 1944. It was indeed the first death camp liberated by the Allies, and would turn out to be one of the best-preserved camps of the Holocaust because the Russian advance was so fast.

The Russians took photographs and even motion pictures of the camp. These were the first images of concentration camps the world would ever see. These images were especially horrible to those who had never heard of a concentration camp, had no idea they existed, or could even believe it if they had been told about them.

Rachel and Ivan walk past the bodies of the dead Nazi guards lying still on the grass. It doesn't take long for them to encounter an area with about a dozen cots and scrawny prisoners lying in them.

Nurses in white hats are trying to save these poor people. A kettle of hot water is set up. The nurses are spoon-feeding the prisoners water.

In fact, all of them will die despite efforts to save them. The nurses would have been better off attending others who were not beyond hope, Rachel would later comment.

Rachel and Ivan head a little deeper inside the camp. They come to some wooden barracks and enter one. There are rows of wooden beds without even straw for the people to sleep on, with many people squeezed into each bed, barely alive. Other people stand listlessly all around, waiting for.no one really knows.

Ivan and Rachel have a couple slices left of the bread they brought. They take them out and offer them to the inmates. Suddenly, they are surrounded by about twenty starving prisoners. They give everyone a little piece.

As they eat, Rachel asks, "What happened here? What is this place?"

"This place is Hell," one of the prisoners said.

How true.

Rachel tries to start other conversations, but the prisoners don't have the physical or mental strength to even talk. Ivan and Rachel stay with them a short while and then leave. They continue walking deeper inside the camp.

After a short while they come to a building that was partially destroyed. The crematorium.

When the end was near, the Nazis blew up the crematoria in Majdanek. It was a futile attempt to hide their crime, and only solidified the fact that they were aware of their guilt.

When Rachel arrives there, the main building with its ovens is mostly intact. As horrified as she is, she senses at that moment that she is an eyewitness to history. She has to witness this and tell the world.

At the time, however, she cannot speak. There are no words. She cannot even cry. There are no tears.

"I've seen enough," Rachel tells Ivan. "Now I have to go home."

CHAPTER 43

WHERE IS HOME?

AFTER A BRIEF STAY IN LUBLIN, RACHEL AND THE ROLUKS RETURN TO Ludmir. There is a lot of cleaning up to do. The Germans ransacked the Roluks' home, and their fields were burned. It will take a long time to rebuild.

Rachel pitches in and does whatever she can to help. She has nothing else to do and no other place to go.

One day, a Ukrainian neighbor tells the Roluks of Jewish survivors congregating in Poland. Some, rumor has it, are even talking about starting a new life in Palestine. Others speak about the United States.

It's all too much for Rachel to absorb. She doesn't know what to do, so she finds comfort in details — working on all the specifics necessary to help the Roluks get their house, farm, and lives back in order.

Meanwhile, tragedy strikes the Roluk home. Soviet soldiers come and arrest Stephan. Others informed on him that he worked for the SS. No amount of explaining helps and he is sent to Siberia.

The Soviets under Josef Stalin didn't need an excuse to execute and imprison their own citizens. Even Soviet prisoners of war — Russian soldiers who fought against the Nazis and put their lives on the line for Stalin — were treated as traitors upon their return to the Soviet Union after the war.

Remarkably, according to some sources, over 1.5 million surviving Red Army soldiers imprisoned by the Germans came home and were immediately sent to Stalin's dreaded Siberian labor camps, for no other reason than they were captured by the Nazis!

Not long after Stephan is taken away, Maria approaches Rachel as she folds some laundry. "Dear Rachel, I must talk to you and I must speak my mind. I must tell you what is in my heart."

Rachel stands there, numb.

"There is no future for you here," Maria intones.

Rachel continues folding as if she doesn't hear the words, but Maria wants to make sure she has her full attention. "Child, please stop folding and look at me."

Rachel puts down the laundry and slowly turns.

"My child, you're a wonderful girl, and you'll make a fine wife one day. But your future is not with us. Your future is not with me. Your future is with your people."

Rachel tries to hold back tears.

"Yes," Maria continues. "It's with your people. I can fake it. You can fake. We can all fake it. But you have a people. And you're part of them. You must leave here and find yourself, find your future with them."

Rachel begins to cry. Maria puts her arm around her shoulder.

"And you must leave tomorrow. There's rumor that the Russians will close the border and you'll be stuck here forever. You must leave tomorrow and head to Poland. I don't know where you'll go and who you'll meet on the way, but if your God has let you live and come this far, then He will surely have mercy on you and bring you to the place you need to be. I'll prepare a sack of food and some clothes, and tomorrow I'll walk you to the train station. There are a lot of people streaming west, including Jews. May your God bless you and help you find your way."

Rachel puts her head on Maria's shoulder and sobs. Maria pats Rachel on the head and comforts her. "Shh. It'll be all right, child. It'll be all right."

Then Maria walks away.

After she is out of sight, Rachel breaks down and cries the cry of a thousand tears — of six million tears. They are streaming down her cheeks.

Silently, out of sight, Maria cries too.

CHAPTER 44

AWAY FROM HERE

THE NEXT DAY MARIA WALKS RACHEL ALL THE WAY TO THE RAILROAD station. Then she says good-bye and walks away. That was it.

Rachel feels like crumbling. She wants to follow. But she knows she cannot.

She is so afraid.

So alone.

She stands at the tracks with others. There are a few dozen of them. More are walking down the road toward the train station. Rachel looks into their faces, hoping to see a familiar one. Hoping to see a friendly face. But everyone looks like a stranger.

How alone she is.

Suddenly, she hears her name. "Rachel?"

She turns, but there is a sea of faces, none recognizable.

"Rachel Blum," the same voice says.

Then, through the crowd, a woman steps forward. "It is Rachel Blum," she says.

Rachel rubs her eyes. "Rivka?"

"Yes."

"Rivka Wax?"

They hug.

In the distance, they hear the horn blast of a train.

Suddenly, a young man emerges from the crowd next to Rivka. Rachel and the young man look at each other. Then Rivka volunteers, "This is my brother, Yonah." Then, addressing Yonah, "This is Rachel Blum. We met in the ghetto." "Glad to meet you, Rachel," Yonah says in a cute, shy way. "Where are you going?" he asks.

"Away from here," Rachel replies.

"Me too."

EPILOGUE

THE STORY OF RACHEL BLUM *AFTER* THE WAR MERITS AN ENTIRE BOOK unto itself. After Maria Roluk pushed her to join her people, it propelled Rachel in a direction that sparked an entire new set of circumstances and miracles that would lead her to marriage and a family of her own.

Rachel married Yonah Szakamer, brother of Rivka Wax, in one of the displaced persons (DP) camps that Holocaust survivors typically found themselves in after the war. They had a daughter there and eventually received permission to go to the United States in 1951 (where they changed their name to Schatzkamer). There they had two more children.

There were so many people whose stories intertwined with Rachel's, and Rachel found out how only some of those stories ended. Kayla, who had been Rachel's friend in the ghetto for years, managed to link up with partisans in the forest. She cooked for them, cleaned for them, stood guard duty — anything to make herself useful. In this way, she managed to survive the war. Rachel and Kayla met each other after the war and stayed in touch for a while.

Rachel's sister, Hannah, on the other hand, didn't survive the war. She had been staying in the Ludmir ghetto with a family, watching their five-year-old son and newborn. On the day of the liquidation, the family entered their hiding place. But the baby was making noise, so the mother took the baby and left the hiding place. When the murderers entered the apartment, they killed the mother and the newborn. However, in doing so, the others were not discovered. The mother knowingly gave up her life and that of her baby to save the lives of her other child, her husband, and Hannah.

The three escaped the ghetto and found temporary shelter on a non-Jewish farm. Tragically, a Ukrainian farmer informed on them, and they too were murdered. Rachel found out this information only because the Ukrainian farmer -- proud of the absolution his priest had given him — had boasted about this to a friend of the Roluks, who shared the story with Rachel.

~

RACHEL NEVER MADE contact with Maria or any of the Roluks after the war. She never found out if Stephan was ever freed or reunited with his parents.

Rachel lived to see grandchildren and great-grandchildren before she passed away on June 20, 2013. (Rachel never knew her birthday. She believed she was born in 1929, making her eighty-four at the time of her passing, but she didn't know for sure.) She was a tower of strength to her family and friends, and an inspiration to all those she came in contact with.

She was even an inspiration to complete strangers. Whether it was the gardener, mailman, handyman, or doctor, strangers were at ease with her almost instantly. She had a quality that's hard to define, but is captured in the Hebrew word *chein*. Often translated as "favor" or "grace," it's best understood as a "connection that is not visible." Rachel possessed *chein*. She had a way of creating an invisible connection. People were drawn to her cheerful, upbeat, and positive attitude — even those who didn't know of her Holocaust past, which certainly would have won her their sympathy. Consciously or not, they were hooked into Rachel's amazing attitude in life.

∽

I KNEW Rachel Schatzkamer for twenty-eight years. She was my mother-in-law. I married her youngest daughter. But in a sense, I never knew her — certainly not until the last five years of her life.

I knew that she lived through the Holocaust. I knew that she had lost her entire family and was alone in the world against the Nazis. I knew that she had lived through a nightmare more frightening than any bad dream. I knew enough about her life even in my first year of marriage to know that there was something incongruent about a phrase we all heard her repeat often: "Nothing bad ever happened to me."

The first time I heard it, I had to do a double take. Did I hear her correctly?

The more I got to know her, though, the more I realized that it was not just a cliche. My mother-in-law not only said it, but lived it. Somehow, she was always the one raising the spirits of others. I knew that from the early years of my marriage when our family regularly visited her apartment in Brooklyn, and I knew that from seeing her almost daily during the last decade of her life when she moved near us in upstate New York. I knew it, her entire family knew it, her friends knew it, and even the elderly women in the assisted living home she moved into knew it. Even the governor of New York, George Pataki, knew it when he awarded her a prize for her outstanding communal work.

My mother-in-law was the most active, upbeat person imaginable. Her greatness was not merely that she said, "Nothing bad ever happened to me," despite her experiences, but that she lived it.

However, until the last five years of her life, I never really knew what she went through. She had never told me or anyone in her family, for that matter. My wife and her siblings knew nothing about their mother's Holocaust experiences. This was the norm for many, many Holocaust survivors. It was as if there was an unwritten contract between them that went, "You don't ask, and I won't tell."

Then something happened in 2008. I asked my mother-in-law if she could repeat a Holocaust story I once heard her say — the story of how she made the Roluks swear on their Bible that when they find Jews after the war, to rebury her in a Jewish cemetery — and I asked her if I could record it. She agreed. Once she began telling it to me, she began telling me other stories. And others. They kept coming... and coming. I couldn't get her to stop. Not that I wanted her to. But they started pouring out.

Although we loved each other as son-in-law and mother-in-law, I was distant enough yet safe enough for her to tell me things she would never tell her biological children or a nonrelated interviewer. (I asked her several times if she wanted to be interviewed by an official Holocaust organization; she was always strongly against it. She was afraid of her memories and only trusted me to share them.) In short, she opened to me like no one else. After that first time, we continued almost daily for several weeks until I collected hours and hours of recordings.

I stood in awe as each part of her overall story slowly came into sharp focus. It needed to happen slowly because she told her experiences from the inside out — not necessarily chronologically, and often transitioning from one story to the next without warning or explanation. Furthermore, she often assumed that I knew the background of what she was talking about, whether it was regarding her personal history or the history of the Holocaust. I often had to hear her repeat a story or part of it several times over several sessions before I fully grasped what she was saying.

The story that illustrates this best is the train story. One day, as I was rather numbly listening to her segue into a story about a train, I interrupted her and asked, "Wait a second, Bubby. Did I hear you right? Did you just tell me that you killed one thousand Nazi SS soldiers?"

"Yeah," she said matter-of-factly. "What a life," she added with her signature chuckle.

Once after another time delay in my comprehension, I asked, "Wait, Bubby, stop. Did you just say that you were in Majdanek right after it was liberated?"

"Yeah." Chuckle, chuckle. "What a life."

After hours and hours of interviews, a truly incredible story emerged. From growing up in poverty-stricken Poland during the 1930s to witnessing war, getting locked in a brutal Nazi ghetto, smuggling food for herself and her family, hiding in an attic to escape a liquidation that took some 18,000 lives, being taken in by a non-Jewish couple whose son worked for the SS, being confronted by an SS general, and partaking in an incredibly dangerous scheme to escape a train filled with Nazis, my mother-in-law's real-life drama is a case of truth being stranger than fiction, and one packed with nonstop action.

In retelling that story here, I took some minor liberties to flesh it out, such as putting dialogue in the mouths of people. The people and situations reflect the reality of the experience my mother-in-law told me, but I have at times expanded upon or even created a conversation.

The story of the Roluks is true, and Ivan Roluk was a train engineer-driver, but his experiences in Treblinka as portrayed in this book were invented to provide historical context of what was happening to Jews elsewhere at the time. (Although, for all we know, it is not implausible that Ivan could have been sent to a death camp to perform the Nazis' bidding at one point.) Wherever I could, I have researched the historical background both to verify for myself and understand better the stories my mother-in-law was sharing.

The result is a vivid account of a teen girl's struggle to survive in a world desperately trying to exterminate her, the true story of an adolescent who answers desperation with ingenuity, suffering with hope. Hers is a story that represents the starkest contrast between two extremes: the weakest and most helpless — a young girl alone — versus the strongest and cruelest — the Nazi state.

Although my mother-in-law emerged the victor, she was not initially the tower of strength she became. Her courage and determination evolved through her experiences. From an isolated, frightened girl, her selfless concern for others not only enabled her to make it through alive but with an unbelievably positive outlook on life, one that to her dying day drew others to her like a magnet. She lost every-

thing yet felt she lacked nothing — to the point that she could
genuinely say, "Nothing bad ever happened to me."

Made in the USA
Middletown, DE
23 April 2019